MW00467314

Faulkner at West Point

Mr. Faulkner, accompanied by Colonel R. K. Alspach, paid an office call on the Academy's Superintendent, Major General W. C. Westmoreland.

U.S. Army Photograph

FAULKNER
AT
WEST POINT

EDITED BY

Joseph L. Fant, III

Major, U.S. Army

AND

Robert Ashley

Lieutenant Colonel, U.S. Army Reserve

*with the assistance of
other members of the English Department,
United States Military Academy*

University Press of Mississippi
Jackson

A publication celebrating the Bicentennial of the United States Military Academy

www.upress.state.ms.us

First published in 1964 by Random House, Inc.
Copyright © 2002 by University Press of Mississippi per Jill Faulkner Summers

Manufactured in the United States of America

10 09 08 07 06 05 04 03 02   4 3 2 1
∞

Library of Congress Cataloging-in-Publication Data

Faulkner, William, 1897–1962.
    Faulkner at West Point / Edited by Joseph L. Fant, III, and
    Robert Ashley, with the assistance of other members of the
    English Dept., U.S. Military Academy.
        p. cm.
    ISBN 1-57806-445-7 (pbk. : alk. paper)
    1. Faulkner, William, 1897–1962—Interviews. 2. Novelists,
American—20th century—Interviews. 3. Southern States—In
literature. 4. Fiction—Authorship. I. Fant, Joseph L. II. Ashley,
Robert Paul, 1915 III. Title.

PS3511.A86 Z524   2001
813'.52—dc21
[B]   2001046688

British Library Cataloging-in-Publication Data available

Pages 7 through 45 contain selections from *The Reivers*, © copyright 1962 by William Faulkner.

Contents

Preface to the Second Edition

Faulkner at West Point and *The Reivers*

William Faulkner's visit to the United States Military Academy at West Point, April 19–20, 1962, just two and a half months before his death on July 6, was one of the writer's last public appearances. It came at a time in his life when he had begun to accept his role as a public figure, a representative of the world of letters. Faulkner's early career was characterized by literary experimentation and reclusiveness, and during those years both his writing and he himself were, as he thought, misunderstood. After receiving the Nobel Prize in 1950, he began to see a change in the way his work was received. Not coincidentally, the tenor of that work was changing too. The modernist experimentation of the thirties was giving way to a more generally liberal, humanistic style, and we see a change in focus from characters who give up or cop out, like Joe Christmas or

Henry Sutpen, to characters who strive to enact change, like Chick Mallison in *Intruder in the Dust*.

Commenting on Faulkner's late style, Michael Millgate suggests that we can see the Nobel Prize acceptance speech as the turning point in the writer's career, after which it is clear that his conception of himself changes. He reflects a new sense of the responsibilities of his position, coming to regard himself as a kind of "elder statesman of letters" (271). In the thirties Faulkner had said that nothing could move him again as much as the sight of Caddy's muddy drawers, the vision at the center of *The Sound and the Fury* (published in 1929). Thus for Millgate, Faulkner's later career is more a matter of "amplification, explication, and affirmation—of reaffirmation, indeed, and even of repetition" of this early, defining vision (272). According to biographer Frederick R. Karl, Faulkner came late in his career to be known as a patriot, as a proponent of democracy and equality who had "transformed his early career as an innovator and avant-garde modernist into an international reputation in which he was completely accepted by those otherwise alien to his sensibility" (1019).

Faulkner came to West Point at the suggestion of his son-in-law Paul D. Summers Jr., a 1951 graduate of the Academy. By all accounts Faulkner was very pleased to have been invited. West Point clearly appealed to his lifelong romance with the military experience. His first novel, *Soldier's Pay*, focusing on a maimed WWI veteran returning home after the war, reflects a pose

Faulkner struck himself on his return to Mississippi after his abortive attempt to join the fighting in Europe. The tragedy and occasionally the vaingloriousness of soldiers at war remained central in his writing throughout his career, framed at the end as it had been at the beginning, as a matter of personal sacrifice impacted by deeply entrenched cultural narratives of violence. His last sustained treatment of these ideas came in *A Fable*, published in 1954, an allegorical work set in France during WWI. Characteristic of Faulkner's writing in his later years, this work comments on the social and political forces at work behind war by focusing on the visions and frustrations of individual soldiers.

For his reading to the Military Academy cadets, however, Faulkner chose passages from a much different kind of work, *The Reivers*, his last novel, published in 1962. Far removed from modernist experimentation or dense religious allegory, this novel has a tone of grandfatherly reminiscence, of quiet, humorous reflection on the idylls of a rural boyhood. An almost self-conscious capstone to a long career, *The Reivers* mines many of the old durable veins of Faulkner's work. Its main plot thread is a perilous journey of adventure and discovery to Memphis, a kind of Paradise and Purgatory of the country imagination. It also involves horse-thieving, race relations, and a young boy's coming of age in the early years of the twentieth century.

The first mention of the idea that will become *The Reivers* appears in a letter to Robert K. Haas, Faulkner's editor at Random House, dated May 3, 1940, in which

Faulkner requests a $1000 advance for a story he says he's interested in writing along the lines of *Huckleberry Finn*:

> A normal boy of about twelve or thirteen, a big, warmhearted, courageous, honest, utterly reliable white man with the mentality of a child, an old Negro family servant, opinionated, querulous, selfish, fairly unscrupulous, and in his second childhood, and a prostitute not very young anymore and with a great deal of character and generosity and common sense, and a stolen racehorse which none of them actually intended to steal. (Blotner 123–24)

According to Karl much of *The Reivers* has an autobiographical shape: like Faulkner, the narrator has worked in a livery stable for his father, has three younger brothers, a servant named Mammie Callie, and a big simpleminded white retainer. "It is," he says, "a familiar temporal collapsing; older man and young boy of eleven, after and before the Fall. It is Faulkner roving in and out of his life and work: dedicating the novel to his grandchildren . . . speaking of himself and his three brothers and their father, and his livery stable" (Karl 1033). Contrasting it with work of the early period of modernist experimentation, Millgate calls *The Reivers* "unmistakably a most genial work, its opening 'Grandfather said' signaling, in combination with its dedication to its author's grandsons, the final erosion of that classically modernist impersonality which as late as *A Fable* Faulkner had struggled to maintain with a rigidity that threatened to turn the book to stone, and himself along with it" (Millgate 273).

The Reivers had not yet come out when Faulkner visited West Point, but Colonel Russell K. Alspach, Head of the English Department, had a prepublication copy in his office, and Faulkner decided he would read from that. It was an interesting choice for an audience of cadets. Far removed from his earlier stories of glory in battle and from his later vision of war as a trammeling master narrative, *The Reivers* focuses on a boy's coming of age, his initiation into the world of adult responsibility. It is, moreover, an affirmative statement about human potential, a contrast to earlier formulations, like "The Bear," in which the possibilities of education and initiation are questioned. In *The Reivers* Faulkner seems to be revisiting old scenes of tragedy and reshaping them, creating forms which will allow him to realize his greater sense of optimism for human fulfillment. John E. Bassett suggests that "in his final years [Faulkner] occasionally spoke as if he were finished writing, as if he were ready to break his pencil; and there is an appropriate finality to *The Reivers* that makes it seem a book intended to round things off, to be a coda to a grandly orchestrated symphony" (53).

We hear in *The Reivers* a voice that is much less ironic, much less distant, much less distorted by technical experimentation and modernist alienation, than most of Faulkner's earlier work, and his decision to read from this work in his address to the cadets at West Point suggests that his intended message was a straightforward one. It is as if Faulkner realizes that this will be one of his last chances to make a public statement and that he wants not only the Corps of Cadets but also the public at large to remember him as an advocate for the human spirit.

David L. G. Arnold
Professor
Department of English
USMA, West Point

Works Cited

Bassett, John E. "*The Reivers*: Revision and Closure in Faulkner's Career." *Southern Literary Journal* XVIII:2 (1986), 53–61.

Blotner, Joseph, ed. *Selected Letters of William Faulkner*. New York: Random House, 1977.

Carothers, James B. "The Road to *The Reivers*." A *Cosmos of My Own: Faulkner and Yoknapatawpha 1980*. Ed. Doreen Fowler and Ann J. Abadie. Jackson: University Press of Mississippi (1981), 95–124.

Millgate, Michael. "Faulkner: Is There a 'Late Style'?" *Faulkner's Discourse: An International Symposium*. Ed. Lothar Hönnighausen. Tübingen: Max Niemeyer Verlag (1989), 271–75.

Introduction

When William Faulkner accepted our invitation to come to West Point, we made all arrangements for a complete record of his visit.

On April 20, 1962, just before the departure of the Faulkner party from West Point, Paul D. Summers, Jr., Faulkner's son-in-law, said he felt sure that Mr. Faulkner would consent to our publishing such a record. We are grateful that Mrs. Faulkner and Mrs. Summers have held to this view.

In *Faulkner in the University*—the record of Mr. Faulkner's class conferences at the University of Virginia, 1957–1958—the editors say:

At Mr. Faulkner's suggestion and in his phrasing, we warn the reader that any resemblance the ideas and opinions expressed here have to ideas and opinions Mr. Faulkner has held or expressed previously, and to the ideas and opinions which—since he intends to continue to live and to test and discard for some time yet—he might hold or express in the future, is purely coincidental.[1]

With the exception of a reading from his works at the University of Virginia on May 17 and his visit to New York City on May 24 to accept the Gold Medal of the National Institute of Arts and Letters, the West Point visit was Mr. Faulkner's last public appearance. Hence the views he shared with the cadets represent some of the last opinions he held. It is interesting to juxtapose some of these opinions with those he held four or five years earlier during his tenure as Writer-in-Residence at the University of Virginia as they are reflected in the Gwynn-Blotner text. To facilitate such a comparison, the officers who edited this transcript of tape recordings of Mr. Faulkner's sessions with the cadets have adopted a format similar to that used in *Faulkner in the University*.

Many who knew William Faulkner longer and far better than we did will remember him for different things. We had long admired his literary genius, but in an acquaintance of just about twenty-four hours, we learned to appreciate his innate humility, grace, and dignity. He epitomized those things he liked most about "my country, the South," as he phrased it. We shall not soon forget him.

---

1. Frederick L. Gwynn and Joseph L. Blotner (eds.), University of Virginia Press, 1959, pp. viii–ix.

Our deepest obligations are to Mrs. William Faulkner; and to Mr. and Mrs. Paul D. Summers, Jr., who did much to interest Mr. Faulkner in making the trip. Mr. Robert W. Berry of Malibu, California, a mutual friend of Mr. Summers and Major Joseph L. Fant, also helped.

Russell K. Alspach
Colonel, USA, Professor
Head of Department of English
USMA, West Point

Faulkner at West Point

On February 10, 1962, William Faulkner accepted the invitation of Major General W. C. Westmoreland to speak at West Point on the evening of April 19, 1962.

The Faulkner party—Mr. and Mrs. Faulkner and Mr. and Mrs. Paul D. Summers, Jr., of Charlottesville, Virginia—landed at Stewart Air Force Base near Newburgh, New York, about noon April 19. The party was driven from Stewart Field to West Point's Hotel Thayer, where the Presidential Suite had been reserved for Mr. and Mrs. Faulkner. After lunch Mr. Faulkner and Mr. Summers walked (Mr. Faulkner preferred throughout his visit to walk although a car was available for his use) the three-quarters of a mile to the Academy's main academic building, Thayer Hall. In the office of Colonel Alspach they had coffee and chatted with several members of the department. Mr. Faulkner said little, and that in a rather soft and low voice. He did, however, make a culinary comment about the coffee, "I make my coffee at home in an old lard bucket that I haven't cleaned for twenty years. I put some coffee and water in, boil it for a while, and that's coffee."

Since it had been agreed that he would not lecture but rather would read briefly from his works and then answer cadet questions, a conversation continued that had begun earlier among Mr. Summers, Summers's USMA classmate Major Fant, and Mr. Faulkner about which of his works he would read from. A copy of his latest work *The Reivers* (a pre-publication copy made available by Random House) was on Colonel Alspach's desk. He handed it to Mr. Faulkner, whose face lighted up as he said, "I haven't seen this yet, sir. May I borrow this to read from tonight?" Colonel Alspach of course agreed, but smiled and said he was lending it to Mr. Faulkner only if Mr. Faulkner would autograph it. "I'd be glad to, sir."

Mr. Summers asked Mr. Faulkner if he knew what the new book was selling for. He replied that he didn't and he was told, $4.95. This perhaps prompted a later comment by Mr. Faulkner after he noticed a bookcase of paperbacks used by cadets for collateral reading. "Paperbacks are fine," he said, "but none of them should cost more than twenty-five cents."

The Faulkner party; the President of Sarah Lawrence College and his wife, Dr. and Mrs. Paul L. Ward; the Dean of the Academic Board of the Military Academy and his wife, Brigadier General and Mrs. William W. Bessell; and a few members of the West Point faculty were guests of General and Mrs. Westmoreland at dinner before the lecture, or "reading." The party then went to the South Auditorium (Mr. Faulkner was told no one would think of asking him to speak in the *North* Auditorium) of Thayer Hall for the talk.

General Westmoreland introduced Mr. Faulkner to the audience of over 1400 that included about 1000 cadets. Mr. Faulkner responded:

Thank you, General Westmoreland. Gentlemen of the faculty, staff, gentlemen of the Corps, ladies and gentlemen, I have been given permission to read from the book that I have just finished. I will have to skip about a little to read about a horse race which to me is one of the funniest horse races I ever heard of. The people concerned are an eleven-year-old white boy named Lucius Priest, a fourteen- or fifteen-year-old Negro boy named McWillie, and two horses—one is a thoroughbred which has been frightened and spoiled called Acheron; the other is a three-quarters, maybe seven-eighths, bred horse that simply won't run. The main character in this is a Negro man named Ned, who thinks he can make this horse run.

———————

The following transcript of Mr. Faulkner's reading from *The Reivers* is published because the reading was not a literal repetition of the printed text of the novel. Mr. Faulkner doubtless intended some of his interpolations to bridge the gap over omitted sections of the printed text, and others to provide necessary explanatory material for an audience which had not read the novel, and could not have read it, since it had not been officially released: these interpolations are set off in brackets. Other interpolations were probably owing to the inevitable differences between an oral and a written presentation, and a few were probably simply misreadings. But one wonders how many of the interpolations in the two latter groups reveal the never-satisfied artist reworking and reshaping his work even after it has received its supposedly final form, for as Mr. Faulkner himself said, "no writer is ever quite satisfied with the work he has done." The interpolations in these latter two groups are printed above the lines of the text of the novel as published.

William Faulkner

Reading from *The Reivers*

South Auditorium, Thayer Hall

Thursday Evening, April 19, 1962

———

[They have got to the paddock near the race track—it's

a half-mile track.]

"Here come the other horse,"

~~"Here they come,"~~ Sam said. "We aint got time

now. Gimme your foot." ⌃ He threw me up. So we

I gave him my foot and

didn't have time, for Ned to instruct me further or for

anything else. But we didn't need it; our victory in the

first heat (we didn't win it; it was only a dividend

(7)

which paid off later) was not due to me or even to Lightning, [Lightning is the name of this horse which doesn't like to run] but to Ned and McWillie; I didn't even really know what was happening until afterward. Because of my (indubitable) size and (more than indubitable) inexperience, not to mention the unmanageable state toward which the other horse was now well on his way, it was stipulated and agreed that we should be led up to the wire by grooms, and there released at the word Go. Which we did (or were),
beginning to behave
Lightning ~~behaving~~ as he always did when Ned was near enough for him to nuzzle at his coat or hand, Acheron behaving as (I assumed, having seen him but that once) he always did when anyone was near his
and
head, skittering, bouncing, snatching the groom this

(8)

way and that but gradually working up to the wire; it

would be any moment now; it seemed to me that I

actually saw the marshal-murderer fill his lungs [Oh

this is, this is the homemade horse race. This man who

is track marshal is under indictment for murder] . . .
to fill his lungs
                    to holler Go! when I don't know what

happened, I mean the sequence: Ned said suddenly:

"Set tight," and my head, arms, shoulders and all,

snapped; I dont know what it was he used—awl, ice

pick, or maybe just a nail in his palm, the spring, the

leap; the voice not hollering Go! because it never had,

hollering instead:

"Stop! Stop! Whoa! Whoa!" which we—Light-

ning and me—did, to see Acheron's groom still on his

knees where Acheron had flung him, and Acheron and McWillie already at top speed going into the first turn, McWillie sawing back on him, wrenching Acheron's whole neck sideways. But he already had the bit, the marshal and three or four spectators cutting across the ring to try to stop him in the back stretch, though they might as well have been hollering at Sam's cannonball limited between two flag stops. But McWillie had slowed him now, though it was ~~now~~ still a matter of mere choice: whether to come all ~~on~~ around the track or turn and go back, the distance being equal, McWillie (or maybe it was Acheron) choosing the former, Ned murmuring rapidly at my ~~knee~~ face now:

"Anyhow, we got one extra half a mile on him.

This time you'll have to do it yourself because them judges gonter—" They were; they were already approaching. Ned said: "Just remember. This un dont matter nohow—" Then they ~~did~~ disqualified him. Though they had seen nothing: only that he had released Lightning's head before the word Go. So this time I had a volunteer from the crowd to hold Lightning's head, McWillie glaring at me while Acheron skittered and plunged under him while the groom gradually worked him back toward position. And this time the palm went to McWillie. You see what I mean? Even if Non-virtue knew nothing about back-country horse racing, she didn't need to: all necessary was to supply me with Sam, to gain that extra furtherance in evil by some primeval and insentient proc-

(11)

ess like osmosis or maybe simple juxtaposition. I didn't even wait for Lightning to come in to the bridle, I didn't know why: I brought the bit back to him and (with no little, in fact considerable, help from the volunteer who was mine and Lightning's individual starter) held so, fixed; and sure enough, I saw the soles of Acheron's groom's feet and Acheron himself already two leaps on his next circuit of the track, Lightning and me still motionless. But McWillie was on him by this time, before he reached the turn, so that the emergency squad could not only reached the back stretch first but had even stopped and caught Acheron and led him back. So our—mine and Ned's—net was only six furlongs, and the last one of them debatable. Though our main gain was McWillie; he was not just mad

(12)

now, he was scared too, glaring at me again but with more than just anger in it, two grooms holding Acheron now long enough for us to be more or less in position, Lightning and me well ~~to~~ on the outside to give them room, when the word Go came.

And that's all. We were off, Lightning strong and willing, every quality you could want in fact except eagerness, his brain not having found out yet that this was a race, McWillie holding Acheron back now so that we were setting the pace, on around the first lap, Lightning moving slower and slower, confronted with all that solitude, until Acheron drew up and passed us despite all McWillie could do; whereupon Lightning also moved out again, with companionship now, around the second lap and really going now,

Acheron a neck ahead and our crowd even beginning

to yell ~~now~~ as though they were getting their money's

worth; the wire ahead now and McWillie, giving

Acheron a terrific cut with his whip, might as well

have hit Lightning too; twenty more feet, and we

would have passed McWillie on simple momentum.

But the twenty more feet were not there, McWil-

lie ~~giving~~ gave me one last glare over his shoulder of rage

and fright, but triumph too now as I slowed Lightning

and turned him and saw it: now not a fight but rather a

turmoil, . . .

[The finish, the end. That was the first heat. This

was a three-heat race.]

So once more, in the clutch of our respective

starting grooms, McWillie and I sat our skittering and

jockeying mounts behind that wire. (That's right, skittering and jockeying, Lightning too; at least he had learned—anyway remembered from yesterday—that he was supposed to be at least up with Acheron when the running started, even if he hadn't discovered yet that he was supposed—hoped—to be in front when it stopped.)

This time Ned's final instructions were simple, explicit, and succinct: "Just remember, I knows I can make him run once, ~~and~~ I believes I can make him run twice. Only, we wants to save that once I *knows*, until we knows we needs it. So here's what I want you to do just for this first heat: Just before them judges and such hollers Go! you say to yourself *My name is Ned William McCaslin* and then do it."

"Do what?" I said.

"I dont know yet neither," he said. "But Akrum is a horse, and with a horse anything can happen. And with a nigger boy on him, it's twice as likely to. You just got to watch and be ready, so that when it do happen, you done already said *My name is Ned William McCaslin* and then do it and do it quick. And dont worry. If it dont work and dont nothing happen, I'll be waiting right ~~there~~ here at the finish, where I come in. Because we knows I can make him run once."

Then the voice hollered Go! and our grooms sprang for their lives and we were off (as I said, we had drawn this time and McWillie had the pole). Or McWillie was off, that is. Because I dont remember: whether I had planned it or just did it by instinct,

(16)

so that when McWillie broke, I was already braced and Lightning's first spring rammed him into the bridle all the way up to my shoulders, bad hand and all. Acheron already in full run and three lengths ahead when I let Lighting go, but I still kept the three-length gap, both of us going now but three horses apart, when I saw McWillie do what you call nowadays a double-take: a single quick glance aside, using only his eyeballs, expecting to see me of course more or less at his knee, then seeming to drive on at full speed for another stride or so before his vision told his intelligence that Lightning and I were not there. Then he turned, jerked his whole head around to look back and I remember still the whites of his eyes and his open mouth; I could see him sawing frantically at

Acheron to slow him; I sincerely believe I even heard him yell back at me: "Goddammit, white boy, if you gonter race, race!" the gap between us closing fast now because he now had Acheron wrenched back and crossways until he was now at right angles to the course, more or less filling the track sideways from rail to rail ~~it looked like~~ and facing the outside rail and for that moment, instant, second, motionless; I am convinced that McWillie's now frantic mind actually toyed with the idea of turning and running back until he could turn again with Lightning in front. Nor no premeditation, nothing: I just said in my mind *My name is Ned William McCaslin* and cut Lightning as hard as I could with the switch, pulling his head until over ~~so that~~ when he sprang for the gap between

(18)

Acheron's stern and the inside rail, we would scrape Acheron; I remember I thought *My leg will be crushed* and I sat there, the switch poised again, in complete detachment, waiting in nothing but curiosity for the blow, shock, crack, spurt of blood ~~and~~ or bones or whatever it would be. But we had just exactly room enough or speed enough or maybe it was luck enough: not my leg but Lightning's hip which scraped across Acheron's buttocks: at which second I cut again with the switch as hard as I could. Nor any judge or steward, dog trainer, market hunter ~~or~~ nor murderer, nor purist ~~or~~ stickler of the most finicking and irreproachable, to affirm it was not my own mount I struck; in fact, we were so inextricable at that second that, of the four of us, only Acheron actually knew who had been hit.

Then on. I mean, Lightning and me. I didn't—
couldn't—look back yet, so I had to wait to learn what
happened. They said that Acheron didn't try to jump
the rail at all: he just reared and fell through it in a
kind of whirling dust of ~~white~~ planks, but still on his
feet, frantic now, running more or less straight out into
the pasture, spectators scattering before him, until
McWillie wrenched him around; ~~and~~ they said ~~that~~
this time McWillie actually set him quartering at the
fence (it was too late now to go back to the gap ~~in it~~
he had already made; we—Lightning—were too far
ahead by this time) as though he were a hunter. But
he refused it, running instead at full speed along the
rail, but still on the outside of it, the spectators hollering ~~and~~ leaping like frogs from _∧in front ~~of him~~ as he

out

(20)

cleared his new path or precedent. That was when I began to hear him again. He—they: McWillie and Acheron—was closing fast now, though with the outside rail between us: Lightning with the whole track to himself now and going with that same fine strong rhythm and reach and power to which ~~it~~ he had simply not occurred yet that there was any hurry about it; in the back stretch now and Acheron, who had already run at least one extra fifty yards and would have to run another one before he finished, already abreast of us beyond the rail; around the far turn of the first lap now and now I could actually see McWillie's desperate mind grappling frantically with the rapidly diminishing choice of whether to swing Acheron wide enough to bring him back through his self-made gap ~~and~~ onto

(21)

the track again and have him refuse its jumbled wreck-age, or play safe and stay where they were in the new track which they had already cleared of obstacles.

Conservation
~~Conservatism~~ won (as it should and does); again the back stretch (second lap now); now the far turn (second one also) and even on the outside longer curve, they were drawing ahead; there was the wire and Acheron a length at least ahead and I believe I thought for an instant of going to the whip just for the looks of the thing; on; our crowd ~~was~~ yelling now and who could blame them? few if any had seen a heat like this before between two horses running on opposite sides of the rail; on, Acheron still at top speed along his path as empty and open for him as the path to heaven; two lengths ahead when we—Lightning—

passed under the wire, and (Acheron: evidently he liked running outside) already into his third lap when McWillie dragged him by main strength away and into the pasture and into a tightening circle which even he could no longer negotiate. And much uproar behind us now: shouts: "Foul! Foul! No! No! Yes! No heat! No heat! Yes it was! No it wasn't! Ask the judge! Ask Ed! What was it, Ed?"—that part of the crowd which Acheron had scattered from the outside rail now pouring across the track through the shattered gap to join the others in the infield; I was looking for Ned; I thought I saw him but it was Lycurgus, trotting up the track toward me until he could take Lightning's bit, already turning him back.

So I had ~~to get~~ my first information about what had happened ~~(and was still happening too)~~ from hearsay—what little Lycurgus had seen before Ned

sent him to meet me, and from others ~~later before~~
himself
Ned ^came up:

(. . . I had not learned yet that no horse ever walked

to post, provided he was still on his feet when he got
so Ned came up
there, that somebody didn't bet on), ~~coming~~ once or
him
twice almost to blows, with ~~Ned~~ in the center of
until he told me what was going on, the people
it, ~~in effect the crux of it, polite and calm but dogged~~
saying:
~~and insistent too, rebutting each attack.~~ "It wasn't a

race. It takes at least two horses to make a race, and one
them   said
of ~~these~~ wasn't even on the track." And Ned:
                                              ^

"No sir. The rule book dont mention how many
then
horses. It just talks about one horse at a time: ~~that~~ if

it dont commit fouls and dont stop forward motion

and the jockey dont fall off and it cross the finish line
(24)

first, it wins." Then another:

that

"Then you just proved yourself that ^that black won:

it never fouled nothing but about twenty foot of that

fence and it sho never stopped forward motion be-

cause I myself seen at least a hundred folks barely get

out from under it in time and you yourself seen it

pass that finish line a good two lengths ahead of that

"What we'll do,

chestnut." [Until finally they decided,]

is to

"Gentlemen, ~~let me~~ offer a solution. ~~As~~ this

man — ~~meaning Ned~~ — says, his horse ran according

to the rules and went under the wire first. Yet we all

saw the other horse run the fastest race and was in

owner

the lead at the finish. The ~~owners~~ of the horses are

these gentlemen right here behind me: Colonel Lins-

comb, your neighbor, and Mr van Tosch from Mem-

(25)

phis, near enough to be your neighbor too when you

get to know him better. They have agreed, and your

that
judges will approve it, ~~to put~~ this heat that was just

which the bankers—will be put into
run, into^what the bankers call escrow. You all have

and you know what escrow means.
done business with bankers ~~whether you wanted to or~~

~~not" they said he even paused for the guffaw, and~~

~~got it "and you know how they have a name for~~

~~everything "~~

~~"Interest on it too," a voice said, and so he got~~

~~that guffaw free and joined it.~~

~~"What escrow means this time is, suspended.~~

That this—
~~Not abolished or cancelled: just suspended.~~^The bets

still stand just as you made them; nobody won and

nobody lost; you can increase them or hedge them

or whatever you want to; the stake money for the last

heat still stands and the owners are already adding ~~an-~~ up

other fifty a side for the next heat, the winner of this

~~next~~ heat to be the winner of ~~the one that was just~~ all.

~~run.~~ Win this next heat, and win ~~all.~~ everything. What do you

say?" [So that's what they agreed on.]

[They go back to the wire again for the heat that

will settle everything.] . . . ~~So I did and~~ we went

on ~~and so~~ back for the third time McWillie and I crouched

our poised thunderbolts behind that wire. McWillie's

starting groom having declined to be hurled to earth

three times, and nobody else either volunteering or

even accepting conscription, they used a piece of cot-

ton-bagging jute stretched from rail to rail in the

hands of two more democrats facing each other across

the track. It was probably the best start we had had

yet. Acheron, who had thought nothing of diving

through a six-inch plank, naturally wouldn't go within

that fine string
six feet of ~~it,~~ and Lightning, though ~~with~~ his nose

touched
almost ~~touching~~ it, was standing as still as a cow now,

I suppose scanning the crowd for Ned, when the starter

hollered Go! and the string dropped and in the same

second Acheron and McWillie shot past us, McWil-

lie shouting almost in my ear:

"I'll learn you this time, white boy!" and already

gone, though barely a length before Lightning pulled

obediently up to McWillie's knee—the power, the

rhythm, everything in fact except that still nobody had

that
told his head yet this was a race. And, in fact, for the

first time, at least since I had participated, been a

were   looking
factor, we ∧even ~~looked~~ like a race, the two horses as

(28)

though bolted together and staggered a little, ~~on into~~ onto

the back stretch of the first lap, our relative positions,

in relation to our forward motion, changing and alter-

ing with almost dreamlike indolence, Acheron draw-

ing ahead until it would look like he really was about

to leave us, then Lightning would seem to notice the

gap and close it. It would even look like a challenge;

I could hear them along the rail, who didn't really

know Lightning yet: that he just didn't want to be

that far back by himself; on around the back turn and

into the home stretch of the first lap and I give you my

word Lightning came into it already looking for Ned;

I give you my word he whinnied; going at a dead run,

he whinnied: the first time I ever heard a horse nicker

while running. I didn't even know they could.

I cut him as hard as I could. He broke, faltered,

sprang again; we had already made McWillie a present

of two lengths so I cut him again; we went into the

second lap two lengths back and traveling now on the

peeled switch until the gap between ~~him~~ us and Acheron

replaced Ned in what Lightning called his mind, and

he closed it again until his head was once more at

McWillie's knee, completely obedient but not one now

inch more—this magnificently equipped and organised

organisation whose muscles had never been informed

by their brain, or whose brain had never been informed

by its outposts of observation and experience, that the

sole aim and purpose of this entire frantic effort was

to get somewhere first. McWillie was whipping now,

so I didn't need to; he could no more have drawn

do   —he could

away from Lightning than he could have dropped

behind him, through the back stretch again and ~~around~~ through

the back turn again, me still on Lightning and Light-

ning still between the rails, so all that remained from

here out were Ned's final instructions: to pull, ease

him out, presenting McWillie again with almost an-

other length, until nothing impeded his view of the

track, the wire, and beyond it. He—Lightning—even

saw Ned first. The first I knew was that neck-snapping

surge and lunge as though he—Lightning—had burst

through some kind of invisible band or yoke. Then I

saw Ned myself, maybe forty yards beyond the wire,

small and puny and lonely in the track's vacancy while

Acheron and McWillie's flailing arm ~~fled~~ vanished rapidly back of

~~to~~ us; then McWillie's wrung face for an instant too,

(31)

then gone ~~too~~; the wire flashed overhead. "Come on, son," Ned said. "I got it."

He—Lightning—almost unloaded me stopping, cutting back across the track ~~(Acheron was somewhere close behind us, trying I hoped to stop too)~~ and went to Ned at that same dead run, bit bridle and all notwithstanding, and simply stopped running, his nose already buried in Ned's hand, and me up around his ears grabbing at whatever was in reach, sore hand too. "We did it!" I ~~said,~~ cried. "We did it! We beat him!"

"We done this part of it," Ned said. "Just hope to your stars it's gonter be enough."

[Now that was the second [1] heat.]

"Now," Grandfather told Ned, "begin at the beginning."

[1] Editors' note: This was actually the completion of the third heat.

"Wait," Colonel Linscomb said. He leaned and poured whiskey into a glass and held it out toward Ned. "Here," he said.

"Thank you kindly," Ned said. But he didn't drink it. He set the glass on the mantel and sat ~~down~~ again. He ~~had~~ never looked at Grandfather and he didn't now: he just waited.

"Now," Grandfather said.

"Drink it," Colonel Linscomb said. "You may need it." So Ned took the drink and swallowed it at one gulp and sat holding ~~the~~ an empty glass, still not looking at Grandfather.

"Now," Grandfather said. "Begin—"

"Wait," Mr van Tosch said. "How did you make that horse run?"

Ned sat perfectly still, the empty glass motionless

in his hand while we watched him, waiting. Then he

said, addressing Grandfather for the first time: "Will

these white gentlemen excuse me to speak to you
in
private?"

"What about?" Grandfather said.
    You'll
"~~You will~~ know," Ned said. "If you thinks they
                           'em
ought to know too, you can tell ~~them~~."

Grandfather rose. "Will you excuse us?" he said.

He started toward the door to the hall.

"Why not the gallery?" Colonel Linscomb said.

"It's dark there; better for conspiracy or confession

either." So we went that way. I mean, I was already

up too. Grandfather paused again. He said to Ned:

"What about Lucius?"

"He used to it too," Ned said. "Anybody got a right to know what his benefits is." We went out onto the gallery, into the darkness and the smell of the roses and the honeysuckle too, beside the mockingbird which was in a tree not far away, we could hear two whippoorwills and, as always at night in Mississippi and so in Tennessee wasn't too different, a dog barking. "It was a sour dean," Ned said quietly.

"Dont lie to me," Grandfather said. "Horses dont eat sardines."

"This one do," Ned said. "You was there and saw it. Me and Lucius tried him out beforehand. But I didn't even need to try him first. As soon as I laid eyes on him last Sunday, I knowed he had the same kind of sense my mule had."

"Ah," Grandfather said. "So that's what you and

Maury used to do ~~to~~ ^{with} that mule."

"No sir," Ned said. "Mr Maury never knowed about
it neither. Nobody knowed it but me and that mule.

This horse was just the same. When he run that last

lap this evening, I had that sour dean waiting for

him and he knowed it."

[So they go back inside where they're still plot-

ting.]
And Mr van Tosch says,
"Can you make him run again, Ned?"

"I made him run that time," Ned said.

"I said, again," Mr van Tosch said. They sat
to Grandfather
there. "Priest," Mr van Tosch said, "do you believe
                                          ∧
he can do it again?"

"Yes," Grandfather said.

(36)

"How much do you believe it?" They sat there.

"Are you addressing me as a banker or a what?" Grandfather said.

"Call it a perfectly normal and natural northwest Mississippi countryman taking his perfectly normal and natural God-given and bill-of-rights-defended sabbatical among the fleshpots of southwestern Tennessee," Colonel Linscomb said.

"All right," Mr van Tosch said. "I'll bet you Coppermine [1] against Ned's secret, one heat of one mile. If Ned can make Coppermine beat that black of Linscomb's again, I get the secret and Coppermine is yours. If Coppermine loses, I dont want your secret —you can have Coppermine and you ~~take or~~ leave Coppermine can for five hundred dollars—"

[1] Editors' note: Lightning's real name.

"That is, if he loses, I can have Coppermine for five hundred dollars, or if I pay you five hundred dollars, I dont have to take him," Grandfather said.

"Right," Mr van Tosch said. "And to give you a chance to hedge, I will bet you two dollars to one that Ned cant make him run again." They sat there.

"So I've either got to win that horse or buy him
in spite of ~~anything~~ everything I can do," Grandfather said.

"Or maybe you didn't have a youth," Mr van Tosch said. "But try to remember one. You're among friends here; try for a little while not to be a banker. Try," They sat there.

"Two-fifty," Grandfather said.

"Five," Mr van Tosch said.

"Three-fifty," Grandfather said.

"Five," Mr van Tosch said.

"Four-and-a-quarter," Grandfather said.

"Five," Mr van Tosch said.

"Four-fifty," Grandfather said.

"Four-ninety-five," Mr van Tosch said.

"Done," Grandfather said.

~~"Done," Mr van Tosch said.~~

So for the fourth time McWillie on Acheron and I on Lightning (I mean Coppermine) skittered and jockeyed behind that taut little frail jute string. McWillie wasn't speaking to me at all now; he was frightened and outraged, baffled and determined; he knew that something had happened yesterday which should not have happened; which in a sense should not have happened to anyone, certainly not to a nineteen-year-old boy who was simply trying to win

(39)

what he had thought was a simple horse race: no holds

barred, of course, but at least a mutual agreement that

nobody would resort to necromancy. We had not

drawn for position this time. We—McWillie and I—

had been offered the privilege, but Ned said at once:

"Nemmine this time. McWillie needs to feel better

after yesterday, so let him have ~~the~~ his pole where he can

start feeling better now."

So

We were off, McWillie as usual two strides out

before Lightning seemed to notice we had started, and

pulled quickly and obediently ~~up~~ back until he could more

or less lay his cheek against McWillie's knee (in case

he wanted to), near turn, back stretch, mine and

McWillie's juxtaposition altering, closing ~~and~~ opening

with that dreamlike and unhurried quality probably

quite familiar to people who fly aeroplanes in close

formation; far turn and into the stretch for the first

lap, I by simple rote whipping Lightning onward ~~about~~ until

one stride before he would remember to begin to look

for Ned; I took one quick raking glance at the faces

along the rail looking for Ned's and Lightning ran

that whole stretch not watching where he was going

at all but scanning the rush of faces for Ned's, like-

wise in vain; near turn again, the back stretch again

~~and~~ into the far turn, the home stretch; I was already

swinging Lightning out toward the outside rail where

~~(Acheron might be beating us but at least he wouldn't~~

~~obstruct our view)~~ he could see. But if he had seen Ned

this time, he didn't tell me. Nor could I tell him,

Look! Look yonder! There he is! because Ned wasn't

there: only the vacant track beyond ~~the~~ that taut line of the wire as fragile-looking as a filtered or maybe attenuated moonbeam, McWillie whipping furiously now and Lightning responding like a charm, exactly one neck back; if Acheron had known any way to run sixty miles an hour, we would too—one neck back; if Acheron had decided to stop ten feet before the wire, so would we—one neck back. But he didn't. We went on, still paired but staggered a little, as though bolted together; the wire flicked overhead, McWillie and I speaking again now—that is, he was, yelling back at me in a kind of cannibal glee: "Yah-yah-yah, yah-yah-yah," slowing also but not stopping, going straight on (I suppose) to the stable; he and Acheron certainly deserved ~~to~~ it. I turned Lightning and walked back. to Ned

who
was trotting toward us, Grandfather behind him

though not trotting; our sycophants and adulators of

yesterday had abandoned us; Caesar was not Caesar

now.

"Come on," Ned said, taking the bit, rapid but

calm: only impatient, almost inattentive. "Hand—"

"What happened?" Grandfather said. "What the

devil happened?"

"Nothing," Ned said. "I never had no sour dean

for him ~~this~~ that time, and he knowed it. Didn't I tell you

this horse ~~got~~ had sense?" Then to me: "There's Bobo

over yonder waiting. Hand this plug back to him so

he can take it on back to Memphis. We're going home

tonight."

[Now the sequel is a postscript; it happens two days later—they are back home.]

And this is all. It was ~~And this is all. It was~~ ^{On} Monday afternoon, after school (Father wouldn't let Mother write me an excuse, so I had to take the absent ~~marks~~ ^{mark}. But Miss Rhodes was going to let me make up the work) and Ned was sitting on the back steps again, Grandmother's steps this time, but in the shade this time too. I said:

"Well I'm glad we didn't ~~If we'd just thought to~~ bet ~~that~~ money ^{much} ~~Sam~~ ~~gave us~~ on Lightning ~~that~~ last time, ~~we could~~ ^{that sho would} have settled ~~what to do about it good.~~ ^{us}

"~~I~~ ^{It} did settle it ~~good,~~" Ned said. "I got five for three this time. Old Possum Hood's got twenty dollars for his church now."

"But we lost," I said.

"You and Lightning lost," Ned said. "Me and that money was on Akrum."

————

After the applause subsided, Colonel Alspach rose and said that Mr. Faulkner had kindly consented to answer any questions. (In the various transcripts throughout this record of questions and answers, a few of the cadets' questions have been slightly edited to make them more concise, but Mr. Faulkner's answers have been reproduced verbatim from the tape recordings of his remarks. No attempt has been made to reproduce Mr. Faulkner's regional dialect or pronunciation. The punctuation represents the editors' best efforts to clarify Mr. Faulkner's comments. Dashes are used to indicate shifts in thought.)

Transcript of Questions and Answers
following Reading

Q. Sir, in your address upon receiving the Nobel Prize you said it was the writer's "privilege to help man endure by lifting his heart. . . ." How do you believe that you have fulfilled this task in your work?

A. It's possible that I haven't. I think that is the writer's dedication. It's his privilege, his dedication too, to uplift man's heart by showing man the record of the experiences of the human heart, the travail of man within his environment, with his fellows, with himself, in such moving terms that the lessons of honesty and courage are evident and obvious. I think that that's the reason, possibly, the poet, the writer, writes. Whether he's successful or not is something else. Probably the only reason the poet ever writes another poem is that the one he just finished didn't quite serve that purpose—wasn't good enough—so he'll write another one.

Q. Sir, I'd like to know, out of all the works you've written in your time of writing, which one do you personally consider to be your best, and what leads you to this decision?

A. That goes back to the answer I just gave. I think that no writer is ever quite satisfied with the work he has done, which is why he writes another one. If he ever wrote one which suited him completely, nothing remains but to cut the throat and quit. And in my own case, the one that is closest to me would be the one that failed the most, that gave me the most trouble. So no writer can judge what he thinks is the best. It's like the mother with the child who is an idiot or born crippled—that that child has a place in the heart which the hale, strong child never has. That may be true of any writer, that the one that's closest to him is the one he worked the hardest at—the failure which was the most painful failure. So I'd have to answer that question in the—which is the one that cost me the most anguish and that I still don't like the most, which is one called *The Sound and the Fury*.

Q. Sir, you said that, if you had fulfilled your ambitions as a writer, the only thing would be to cut your throat and quit. Do you believe this is the reason that Mr. Hemingway died? Sir, do you believe that he killed himself for this reason, or do you believe that his death was an accidental death?

A. No, I don't. I think that Hemingway was too good a man to be victim of accidents; only the weak are victims of accidents unless a house falls on them. I think that that was a deliberate pattern which he followed just as all his work was a deliberate pattern. I think that every man wants to be at least as good as what he writes. And I'm inclined to think that Ernest felt that at this time, this was the right thing, in grace and dignity, to do. I don't agree with him. I think that no man can say until the end of his life whether he's written out or not. Probably that occurs to almost everybody at some time, that he has done his best, that this is when he would like to write *finis* to his life. I think that Hemingway was wrong.

Q. Sir, in your novel *Absalom, Absalom,* what is your purpose in relating Colonel Sutpen's story through Quentin Compson—to reveal the character of Quentin, to portray merely Sutpen, or to just portray the South?

A. The primary job that any writer faces is to tell you a story, a story out of human experience—I mean by that, universal mutual experience, the anguishes and troubles and griefs of the human heart, which is universal, without regard to race or time or condition. He wants to tell you something which has seemed to him so true, so moving, either comic or tragic, that it's worth repeating. He's using his own poor means, which is the clumsy method of speech, of writing, to tell you that story. And that's why he invents involved style, or he invents the different techniques—he's simply trying to tell you a story which is familiar to everyone in some very moving way, a way so moving and so true that anyone would say, "Why yes—that's so. That happens to me, can happen to anybody." I think that no writer's got time to be drawing a picture of a region, or preaching anything—if he's trying to preach you a sermon, then he's really not a writer, he's a propagandist, which is another horse. But the writer is simply trying to tell a story of the human heart in conflict with itself, or with others, or with environment in a moving way. Does that answer?

Q. Sir, what is your opinion of the value of modern literature, of the writing about woman's suffrage and confusion of roles as present in modern literature?

A. I look on them as the tools, the material of the trade; that is, they are the conditions which the writer can use in order to portray the human heart in some simple struggle with itself, with others, or with its environment. The sociological qualities are only, in my opinion, coincidental to the story—the story is still the story of the human being, the human heart struggling. To be braver than it is afraid it might be, to be more honest, to be more compassionate, to be nearer the figure that we mean when we say God than it thinks it might be. This integration, segregation, or the sociological conditions are simply tools which the writer uses in order to show the human heart in the struggle of that dilemma—in the battle which is any story. It's the—the individual meets a crisis, does he lick it or does it lick him? That's all any story comes to.

Q. Sir, once again in your Nobel Prize speech, you stated, "Our tragedy today is a general and universal physical fear so long sustained by now that we can even bear it. There are no longer problems of the spirit. There is only the question: 'When will I be blown up?'"

And I wonder, sir, do you feel that our generation today, the generation we're living in right now, is getting out of this feeling of "When will I be blown up?" less than we were, say, in 1950, when you gave this speech? Do you feel our literature is showing this?

A. I think that the young people have really never believed in that statement, that that was the condition of—a universal condition which is supported more by the older people, that the young people who have felt the same toward the beauty and passion of being alive that I felt when I was twenty-one years old, still feel it. But when I was twenty-one years old, we didn't have that general pessimistic, middle-aged feeling of "When shall I be blown up?" which seems to be in the world today. I don't think it's going to stop anybody from being poets; it's just too bad you've got to carry that load. And that didn't refer to the young people—the young people don't care what the old folks think.

Q. Sir, based on what you just said, do you consider that the present world situation is likely to infuse a new spirit of nationalism into American literature?

A. If a spirit of nationalism gets into literature, it stops being literature. Let me elaborate that. I mean that the problems which the poet writes about which are worth writing about, or composing the music, or painting the pictures are the problems of the human heart which have nothing to do with what race you belong to, what color you are—they're the anguishes, the passions, of love, of hope, of the capacity, the doom of the fragile web of flesh and bone and mostly water, of which we are in articulation, must suffer, stuck together by a little electricity and a world of mostly coincidence, that we can endure it all. Yet there's something in us that makes the individual say, "My anguish is beautiful, it's meaningful," so he writes the poem, he composes the music, he paints the picture not to prove anything, not to defy his fate nor his circumstance, but simply because there is something that is so true and so moving in breathing that he has got to put it down, got to make a record of it. You might say that what drives every poet and writer—he knows that in a short time, three score and ten years, he must pass through the last and final oblivion into nothing, that he is at least going to leave on that wall the scrawl "Kilroy was here." His belief is that his own passions are important, and we must all agree with him. If our own passions, our own problems are not important, then there is no reason to be here. What do we get out of being here?

Q. Sir, I would like to know who your favorite author is.

A. Well, that's a question that really don't make much sense to a writer because the writer is not concerned with who wrote, but what he wrote. To me, anyway, the character, the book is the thing, and who wrote it is not important; and the people that I know and love are Don Quixote, and Sarah Gamp and some of Conrad's people, a lot of Dickens' people, Balzac's people, but not Balzac especially, because I think some of Balzac's writing is bad writing. Some of Conrad's writing is bad writing, but some of Conrad's people that he created are marvelous and endured. So I think that—true of any writer—that he looks on the book and not who wrote it, not who made it.

Q. Sir, in many of your works you deal with perversion and corruption in men. How do you feel this uplifts your readers, exemplified in courage and honor?

A. Well, the easy answer is, it may show them what I don't think they should do, which is easy and glib and meaningless. I think that the reason is that one must show man; the writer, the painter, the musician wants to show man not in his—not when he's dressed up for Sunday, but in all his phases, his conditions; then the very fact that to see man in his base attitudes, his base conditions, and still show that he goes on, he continues, he has outlived the dinosaur, he will outlive the atom bomb, and I'm convinced in time he will even outlive the wheel. He still has partaken of immortality, that the aberrations are part of his history, are part of himself, maybe. But within all that is the same thing that makes him want to endure, that makes him believe that war should be eradicated, that injustice should not exist, that little children shouldn't suffer.

Q. Sir, you say that all works of literature arise from a passion and an agony of the heart. Let's say that you start your life on a river with passion and beauty and agony and, as you go through your life, you are trying to find some goal. What is the path that you find easiest—to withdraw from the river and watch it course by, or to succumb to it, stay with it? Should you withdraw from your emotions or stay with your emotions?

A.   I would say by all means to stay with it, to be a part of it. To never be afraid of dirt or filth, or baseness or cowardice, but try always to be better than that, to be braver, to be compassionate, but not to be afraid of it, not to avoid it. I think that the worst perversion of all is to retire to the ivory tower. Get down in the market place and stay there. Certainly, if you want to be a painter or a writer, maybe if you want to be a philospher, a mathematician, you can get off in a tower, but if you want to be a painter, or a writer, or a poet, you can't be afraid or ashamed—ashamed of your own behavior, not of other people's.

Q.   Sir, at the present time, you seem to have great optimism for the human race, but in some of your earlier writings during the period around the 1920's, this optimism was not too prevalent. Was there any period of life that changed your attitude toward the human race?

A.   No, I wouldn't think so. I would say that this part of the human race which is going steadily on toward a continuation, toward that sort of immortality, are pretty dull folks. The ones that kick up and misbehave and are comic or tragic to me are interesting. But they are not the sum total of the human race. No one lives long enough in three score and ten years to be the human race; he just entered it for a little while—he was a tenant.

Q.   Sir, in the light of the answers you gave to some previous questions, that you believe it's the right and duty of an author to show a character in all its phases in any way that is feasible, what is your stand on present-day censorship?

A.   Well, there should be no such thing as censorship. If the mind has got to be protected by the law from what will harm it, then it can't be very much of a mind to begin with. The first part of your question, can I have that again, please, sir?

Q.   You stated, sir, that you thought it was the right and duty of an author to tell the story of the human heart and its problems. I wonder if you do this and if you do it as *you* see it. You may not see it as others do.

A.   I didn't say it was the right and duty. I think primarily the writer, the artist, works because it's fun. He hadn't found anything that is that much pleasure. He is simply telling a story in the most moving and dramatic way that he can think to do it. He's not following any right nor any duty to improve you; he simply has seen something in the magic and passion of breathing which seems so funny or so tragic that he wants to tell you. And he is trying to tell you in the most moving and economical way he can, so that you will be moved, will laugh or cry, as he did. It's no special right and duty—when he gets involved with right and duty, he's on the verge of becoming a propagandist, and he stops being an artist then. He's doing something simply because he likes it, it's his cup of tea. He'd rather do that than anything else he knows.

Q.   Sir, just where did you get the basis for your characterization of the Snopes and Sartoris families?

A. That's a difficult question to answer. The writer has three sources: one is observation; one is experience, which includes reading; the other is imagination, and the Lord only knows where that comes from. It's like having three tanks on a collector—you open the collector valve, you don't know exactly how much comes from any one tank, so no one can say just where anything comes from—whether he imagined it, whether he saw it or read it or heard it, but you can count on one thing, that the reason they call it fiction is it *is* fiction—that any writer is a congenital liar incapable of telling the truth, and so even he can never say how much he embroidered, imagined anything because he simply could not take any fact he saw and let it alone. He's convinced he can do much better than God could, so he's going to improve it—change it.

Q. Sir, it's been said that literature today tends toward atheism. What's your opinion of this?

A. I don't think so. I think that the literature of today is too much like the literature of all times, which has been the struggle, the history, the record of the struggle of the human heart. What it's struggling toward, a condition, an esoteric condition like atheism or Puritanism or integration or segregation, is not important—it's the battle the heart goes through in trying to be better than it is, to be less cowardly than it is afraid it might be.

Q. Sir, you're described, I believe, as a naturalistic writer. In America, we've progressed quite a ways in naturalism. What work, if you care not to speak about authors, would you describe as furthering naturalism most in America?

A.   To begin with, I don't know what naturalism means. Can you be a little more specific?

Q.   I would say, sir, that we've come a long way since before the 1900's. One of the books that I had in mind was *Sister Carrie* by Theodore Dreiser. And also, works by Sinclair Lewis, I believe, would be described as naturalistic, or naturalistic as opposed to romantic.

A.   Yes, I see what you mean. I still think that the job which the writer is doing is to tell you a moving story of the human heart in conflict. I would say that Dreiser used the best material he had, the best method, the best skill he had, which wasn't very much. He was a bad writer. But he had a tremendous drive to tell you of the conflict of the human spirit. And that's what I meant by saying that I didn't know what a naturalist writer was. That to me, the writer is simply trying to use the best method he possibly can find to tell you a true and moving and familiar old, old story of the human heart in conflict with itself for the old, old human verities and truth, which are love, hope, fear, compassion, greed, lust. He uses naturalism, romanticism as the tools to his hand just as the carpenter uses the hammer or the saw which fits his hand best to trim the board, but he's simply trying to tell you the same story of the human heart in conflict with itself for the eternal verities which haven't changed too much since man first found how to record them.

Colonel Alspach thanked Mr. Faulkner. USMA faculty members commented that the standing ovation given Mr. Faulkner by his audience had rarely been equalled for warmth and depth. Mr. Faulkner stood at the podium and in his courtly manner bowed to the applause.

Later he held a press conference.

Transcript of Questions and Answers during Press Conference

Q. Mr. Faulkner, now that you have completed your question-and-answer session with the West Point cadets, what are your impressions?

A. I am surprised and pleasantly astonished at the things I've found that I didn't expect to find here. I had the layman's notion that this was a stiff, regimented place where robots move to numbers, and I've found it's a little different since I've been here this time.

Q. Didn't you think they seemed very responsive in their questions?

A. I don't know whether I had a selected parade of them, but what I have found here was a—well forward of what I've found at the other schools I have seen. They were in top gear and they knew that they would need to be in top gear and they were. I don't mean racing or running ends, but they were in top gear. In Princeton and Virginia there is something a little sloppy which is not here.

Q. Are you advocating a military background, sir?

A. I'm inclined to think that a military background wouldn't hurt anybody.

Q. I am interested in and was surprised by the cadet reaction to your comment, "If a spirit of nationalism gets into literature, it stops being literature." What made their reaction rather surprising was the fact that their predecessors from this institution, in certain cases, behave as though they think nationalism is a great virtue. Apparently the present student body doesn't.

A. Well, they didn't believe nationalism was a great virtue while they were here. It's only after they got out that they become Edwin Walkers—years after here.

Q. About the young people today compared to your life when you were a youth, do you feel that there's any significant difference?

A. No.

Q. Do you despair of juvenile delinquency?

A. No, there are just more juveniles than there were in my time; they are not more delinquent.

Q. Did you say more juveniles, sir, or more juvenile?

A. There's more juveniles, but they're not any more delinquent.

Q. One of the questions asked was about the younger generation's feeling of getting blown up and whether that feeling had changed since you commented on it when you made your address on winning the Nobel Prize.

A. Well, I still feel that people wonder when I'm going to be blown up, but I still think that ain't very important.

Q. You've advised getting down out of the ivory tower and into the market place. In moving about the market place these days, what distresses you most about contemporary life?

A. You'll have to explain that. I don't know exactly what you mean.

Q. Just generally about contemporary life. Or perhaps what do you despair of most in contemporary life, in moving about the market place?

A. I don't despair of any of it.

Q. What delights you most?

A. What I like best is fox hunting.

Q. The cadets asked also about the perversion and corruption in your novels and how, by this means, you feel that you're uplifting your readers. How is that possible, Mr. Faulkner?

A. Only in—that seems to be a part of the knowledge of human behavior which the artist uses in order to tell you a moving and tragic story of the human heart in conflict with itself, and we assume that the purpose of that conflict is to win even if you have to die with your head still bloody but unbowed.

Q. You repeat that over and over with no embarrassment whatsoever. Is that the one credo that you state over and over again?

A. I would say so, yes. I am convinced that man in time will abolish diseases. It may take a long time, but in time he will abolish war. But I still think he will endure. I think that the last sound on this worthless, fleeting earth will be two people arguing about where they are going next.

Q. Do you find as a writer who has by all means "arrived" that you read as much as you used to?

A. No.

Q. What do you read now?

A. I read the books that I knew and loved when I was twenty-one years old.

Q. Can you tell us some of them?

A. Yes, I go back to the people, not the books—but the people. I like Sarah Gamp—she's one of my favorite people—and Dox Quixote. I read in and out of the Old Testament every year. Shakespeare—I have a portable Shakespeare I'm never too far from.

Q. Is this a form of criticism of contemporary writing or writers?

A. No, it's the glands—the mind has slowed down a little and it don't like new things. It likes the old things just like the old man wants his old shoes, his old pipe. He don't want a new one—the new one's better, he realizes that, but he don't want it. He wants the old one.

Q. And you're simply not interested in contemporary literature, is that it?

A. Not enough to keep up with it. When somebody says, "Here's something you ought to read," I read it. And quite often it's good.

Q. Do you think there are any "up and coming" writers?

A. What do you mean by "up and coming" ones?

Q. Well, are there any good young ones?

A. I am sure there are, that they are still writing. They still must be writing, in Russia and behind all the bamboo and iron curtains.

Q. In our country?

A. I'm sure they are, yes.

Q. Are there any you would recommend?

A. Not until I've read what they write, and I haven't read a—I can't think of a contemporary book I have read in the last, well, since Salinger's *Catcher in the Rye.*

Q. Did you enjoy that?

A. Yes, it was a good book. It was a tragic story of a young man that tried to enter the human race and every time he tried it, it wasn't there. It was a very sad and tragic story.

Q. Was *The Reivers* something that you had wanted to write for a long time?

A. Only the story of the human heart in conflict. Until you have written a perfect one and cut your throat, you keep on trying to write that story.

Q. It's very funny!

A. I think so too. It's one of the funniest books I ever read.

Q. Did you have a good time doing it?

A. Yes, delightful. I wish I hadn't written it so I could do it again.

Q. Mr. Faulkner, do you especially like the scene where they were caught on the road and had to be pulled out by the two mules?

A. Yes, ma'am.

Q. Do you find that writing gets any easier as time goes on? Your writing?

A. I can't answer that question. If you know what you want to say, it's easy to put it down, so I don't know how to answer your question. You mean does it get easy to know what to say? No! No easier, no harder. Some days you know exactly what you want to put down and you put it down—other days you don't.

———————

Mr. Faulkner began his second day at West Point by attending reveille formation, to which, as usual, he walked. A few minutes before that 5:50 A.M. formation, he strolled into the Cadet Guard Room. The senior cadet on duty came to attention and said, "Good morning, Mr. Faulkner, and may I add, sir, how much I enjoyed your talk last night?" Mr. Faulkner was obviously pleased. "Thank you, sir," he replied, "maybe I can do it again some time."

After breakfast at the quarters of Colonel Alspach, Mr. Faulkner and Mr. Summers returned to the hotel. Then at 7:55 A.M., they proceeded to a classroom of Thayer Hall where Mr. Faulkner talked with a section of fifteen fourth-classmen (freshmen) in an advanced English course on The Evolution of American Ideals as Reflected in American Literature. During this session, the power in the air-conditioned, windowless building failed for about twelve minutes. Mr. Faulkner was talk-

ing when the lights went out (and of course to our cha-
grin the tape recorder ceased functioning), but he did
not falter for a moment. Despite the profound darkness, he calmly continued answering questions. A transcript of the tape of this session follows.

EN 152: The Evolution of

American Ideals as Reflected

in American Literature

7:55 A.M.–8:50 A.M., April 20, 1962

Captain James R. Kintz, Assistant Professor of English, USMA: Perhaps I should mention, Mr. Faulkner, that this course is not a survey of American literature; it is a course which explores American ideals as they are reflected in our literature. Recently we have been discussing how the Depression influenced the writers in the early thirties.

Mr. Faulkner: Just so none of the gentlemen expect any conclusions, definite conclusions, about American literature from me—I'm not a very literary man. But I remember the Depression.

Q. Sir, we've read your work "Turnabout." In it you added an additional part to the end. We noticed in your new novel, from which you read last night, that you employed this same technique. Is this technique done to emphasize a certain part, or to summarize, or simply to express a new idea in addition to the work?

A. No, it's done simply through a need. The writer feels that he has got to do this much more in order to underline, emphasize the story he's telling, which, in essence, is simply the story of people in the battles which you constantly face to get through being alive. That's a matter of style, and I am convinced that the story you tell invents its own style, compels its style. That these are not really tricks; they look like tricks and the writer can use the same trick again, but he's not using it because it is a trick—he uses it because it works.

Q. Sir, I was wondering, in the story "Turnabout," there is the young British boy, Midshipman Hope, who actually played World War I as sort of a game—he and his colleagues would count "beavers" every time they'd see a net on a mast, while the American, Captain Bogard, was actually quite conscientious about the war and realized war for what it was, at least he seemed to. Yet the young English boy was killed and the American was not. I wonder if there were actually any conclusions we were to draw from this as to the attitudes that we should have toward the subject of war.

A. No, only the Englishman was only about eighteen or nineteen years old; he should, in normal times, still be in school. The American captain was a mature man—twenty-five or twenty-six. It was not a different attitude—national attitude—toward war; it was a different attitude because of age—of youth and something of maturity. If it showed anything, it showed that possibly the man who was mature might know more how to survive war than a child might. I don't think the story set off to postulate that, but that might be a possible definition of it.

Q. Well, sir, going back to one of the questions that was asked last night, in your acceptance speech of the Nobel Prize you said, "Our tragedy today is a general and universal physical fear so long sustained by now that we can even bear it." And going a step further, in your short story "Turnabout," you picture the American captain in one of the last scenes dive-bombing on a German target, and he wished that all the kings and all the presidents—in effect, all the leaders of the world—were there so that he could wipe them out. Do you feel that this universal fear of this problem in the world today is a cause of our leaders?

A. I don't believe you quite finished—that this universal fear is a cause of our leaders—now finish that. I don't think I understood quite what you meant. That the universal condition has produced the leaders we have, or has compelled the leaders to be not good leaders—which do you mean?

Q. Well, sir, that's what I wondered, actually what you meant. You brought out the fact that we have this universal fear, and then in the story "Turnabout" you create a war situation and you have this American captain, who in effect had everything to live for—he had

had a good life in America—and you have him dive-bombing on a German target and hoping in his own mind that he could wipe out, or wishing in his own mind that he could wipe out, all the kings and generals and presidents. In other words, sir, are the leaders responsible for war?

A. Well, I wouldn't say that, but the leaders are responsible for the clumsiness and the ineptitude with which wars are conducted. War is a shabby, really impractical thing anyway, and it takes a genius to conduct it with any sort of economy and efficiency. I think this man at that moment was—had done the thing that all soldiers in battle at some time have done—to have cursed all the high echelons that got all of us into this to kill some of us. That was something that at that moment he could feel, but it would not be a conviction of his that he would keep always—just at that moment.

Q. Then, sir, this was a universal feeling of the heart that you were bringing out.

A. Yes, that's right. Any soldier would feel that toward the brass safe back in the dugouts and the chateaux that didn't have to run those little boats, or didn't have to ride the aircraft low enough to bomb the chateau.

Q. Sir, last night you stated that the basic goal of an author was to portray the conflict of the human heart. Now, just what do you feel today is the chief trouble with which people are concerned, or should be, and how much has this changed since, let's say in particular, the time of the Depression?

A. I don't think it has changed at all basically. Only the ephemeral symptoms alter—they are not too important. But basically the drives of the heart are the same. It's the verities, for the verities have been the same ever since Socrates, which are courage and pride and honor—compassion. It's man's knowledge that at bottom he is not very brave, that he is not very compassionate, but he wants to be—his conscience—call it what you will, call it God, but he wants to be better than he is afraid that he might be—that he might fail, yet he still tries. I think that is shown in the people that portray incredible courage in battle; that man is fighting too, yet something—we don't know what it is—drove him to do what he himself didn't believe he could; that people show pity—they are the verities which all the writing is about. The temporary conditional things of the time are not too important. At this time, in my country, the South, there is a problem of segregation and integration—racial trouble. But they are not really important in the long view of man's record. At other times, unemployment; at other times, women's rights—they were important ephemerally at the moment, but not important as measured against the passions and hopes of man's heart.

Q. Sir, you said that man's desire to be braver than he really is, more honest and better than he is, has always been the same, and the conflicts of the human heart remain the same. Do you think, sir, that the problems of this age, the increased problems, will have any effect on men's ability to cope with the conflicts within this sort of feeling, and that this will change?

A. It will, I am convinced, to this extent, that man can learn from experience. It takes a lot of it, it takes a long time, but man alone has learned from experience to cope with environment. He's a frail, fragile collection of nerves, and yet he has endured climate, change of temperature. He has survived all the bigger forms of life, and I think that he, in time, he will solve his problems. I think in time he will solve the problem of atomic warfare, of the dread we all live under of being blown up by someone who can buy an installment-plan bomb from some Swiss manufacturer and drop it on somebody he don't like. It will take time, but I am convinced that man is the most durable of all, that he will outlast even his evil.

Q. Sir, I am interested in this hope of man. Hemingway in his early work, especially I'm thinking of his "Snows of Kilimanjaro," pictures man as someone who is disillusioned, who has no real hope, no life to him. Yet in his later work—I'm thinking of *The Old Man and the Sea*—he pictures man as someone with life, with faith, with hope, and with resolution. It seems strange to me that he would kill himself after he seems to have regained a faith in man. I was wondering if you know any possible reason why, after he seems to have regained his faith, he would then decide to take his life.

A. The only reason I would undertake to guess would be that every writer wishes to reduce the sum of all experience, of all the passion and beauty of being alive, into something that will last after him. If he's the first-rate poet, he tries to do it in a quatrain. If he's not a first-rate poet, then he tries to do it in ten pages—he's a short-story writer. If he can't be a short-story writer, then he resorts to eighty thousand words and becomes a third-stage novelist. But he is trying to reduce the passion and beauty that he saw of being alive into something concrete that can be held in the hand, and he fails, and he tries again. I would say that there was a certain point that Ernest reached where he said, "I can't do it, no man can do it, and there's nothing remains worth staying alive for." Or he could have been sick and in pain, and I think that that had something to do with it because he had spent a lot of time in the hospital. The last time I saw him he was a sick man. But I prefer to believe that he had reached that point that the writer must reach—Shakespeare reached it in *The Tempest*—he said, "I don't know the answer either," and wrote *The Tempest* and broke the pencil. But he didn't commit suicide. Hemingway broke the pencil and shot himself.

Q. Sir, you said that the verities haven't changed since the time of Socrates. This seems to be about what you said in your acceptance speech of the Nobel Prize when you said that people are always worrying about the bomb falling on them. It seems now that people are no longer planning far ahead into the future. They think about the pleasure that they can have now because they don't think they can count on what tomorrow will bring. Do you thing that this will cause any change in the basic things that we feel are moral and just?

A. Not really. That is sad and tragic for the generation that had to spend all its time, its waking time, wondering shall I still be alive tomorrow. That is ephemeral—it's too bad for them, but not too bad for the human race because the human race will survive that too. I think that in a few more years there'll be less and less worry about someone dropping that bomb, that in fifty years people will have forgotten—they won't forget the bomb, but they will have forgotten what it felt like to wonder every night when you went to sleep would it fall, would the balloon go up before you could wake?

Q. Sir, you made a lot of mention that man will survive these physical features—his environment and the atom age. Do you think that he will also survive himself and his society with respect to psychological breakdown? It seems as though there has been an awful lot of emphasis on man's mental breakdown—the people in the insane asylums, the number of divorces and suicides, and things of that nature.

A. That is, in my opinion, an ephemeral symptom of the fear which has come about through the new pressures man has invented for himself in this century. There are more nervous breakdowns because there are more things for man to worry about. Also there are more nervous breakdowns because there are more people to break down. That would have something to do with it. But man in his essence in the long view doesn't change. I like to think that he improves gradually—very slowly. The individuals enter the human race and they may break down, collapse, they may make trouble, and they are gone—their tenure is ephemeral. But man himself, in that continuation, I'm convinced, improves. In time, he will get rid of all the evils that he can't cope with—he will get rid of war and disease and ignorance and poverty in time. It may be a long time, and we won't be here to know it, but I'm convinced he will.

Q. Sir, when you feel moved by something so that you want to write about it and make a story out of it, do you write immediately and spontaneously and completely write out the whole story, or is it a gradual process? I'm interested in how you go about writing.

A. There's no rule for that in my case. I'm very disorderly. I never did make notes nor set myself a stint of work. I write when the idea is hot, and the only rule I have is to stop while it's still hot—never to write myself out—to leave something to be anxious to get at tomorrow. Since I have no order, I know nothing about plots. The stories with me begin with an anecdote or a sentence or an expression, and I'll start from there and sometimes I write the thing backwards—I myself don't know exactly where any story is going. I write—I'm dealing simply with people who suddenly have got up and have gotten into motion—men and women who are moving, who are involved in the universal dilemmas of the human heart. Then when I have got a lot of it down, the policeman has got to come in and say, "Now look here, you've got to give this some sort of unity and coherence and emphasis," the old grammatical rules— and then the hard work begins. But it's a pleasure—it's just like you get pleasure out of a hard, fast tennis game—with me, only at some moment the policeman has got to compel the unity and coherence and emphasis to make it a readable story.

Q. Sir, do you ever feel tempted to get your characters out of trouble? Once their characteristics have gotten them into some sort of trouble, do you feel tempted to help them out?

A. I don't have time—by that time, I'm running along behind them with a pencil trying to put down what they say and do.

Q. Sir, thinking of a definition that Tolstoy once had of literature—that good literature was something which taught a good lesson, bad literature was something which taught a bad lesson, and that great literature was something that taught a good lesson that was applicable to all mankind, what is your idea of such a definition?

A. I agree with him absolutely. Only I do think that the writer has not got time to say, "Now, I'm going to teach you a lesson." The writer is saying, "I'm going to tell you a story that is funny or tragic." The lesson is coincidental, even accidental, but all the good books do fall into those categories—he's quite right, I agree with him. But he himself didn't set down to write a book to teach anyone a lesson, I think. He was simply writing about people involved in the passion and hope of the human dilemma.

Q. Sir, in answer to one of the questions last night—I believe it was, "How your portraying more or less perverted characters would help uplift the human heart"—you said that if nothing else it would show that it would be a good idea not to be like these people. I wonder if you ever do portray people who are more or less perverted with the idea of presenting them as unfavorable, or do you just present them just as they are—just as a story about them in the struggle of their heart. Do you ever try to present them as either unfavorable or favorable?

A. Not really. The first thing that a writer has is compassion for all his characters—any other writer's characters. He himself does not feel that he has the power to judge, and these characters, these evils are there. In the story he's telling, it seems to him necessary and good and the best way to tell his story to use this. He doesn't advocate it, he's not condemning it, it's there, and in his clumsy way the first thing he must do is to love all mankind, even when he hates individual ones. Some of the characters I've created, I hate very much, but it's not for me to judge them, to condemn them; they are there, they are part of the scene that we all live in. We can't abolish evil by refusing to mention these people.

Q. Sir, may I ask you one more question along that line? Did you see or do you see Popeye and Joe Christmas as being similar people?

A. Not at all. Popeye was the monster. Joe Christmas, to me, is one of the most tragic figures I can think of because he himself didn't know who he was—didn't know whether he was part Negro or not and would never know.

Q.   Sir, did Popeye have the same problem of not having a society to belong to?

A.   Now I don't understand Popeye. He, to me, was a monster. He was just there.

Q.   Sir, recently in the newspapers and national magazines, there have been several articles about government aid to the artist. I was wondering how do you feel about this?

A.   Why, I would think that the artist ought to get whatever help he can get from any source. All he really needs is a little whiskey and a little tobacco and a little fun. And it don't do him any harm to have to do a little hard work for it, too, but I don't think that a little help is going to ruin the good artist. I don't think that the good artist has got to come from the gutter, either. So whatever he can get from his government, let him take it.

Q.   Sir, then you don't feel that government aid might lead to, say, control of the artist?

A.   Not to the good one. The good one, nobody can control him because he can't control himself. The second-rate one might be turned into a machine, a propagandist, but the first-rate one can't be—nobody can control him, not even himself.

Q.   You spoke just now, sir, of first- and second-rate artists. Now how, exactly, would you separate first- and second-rate authors? Would it be by the trueness or the accuracy of the story which they are telling or just by their style—which one, or both?

A.   It would, in my opinion, be absolutely by the

trueness that they are telling, and I don't mean the sticking to fact because facts and truth don't really have much to do with each other. It's to stick to the fundamental truth of man's struggle within the human dilemma. He can be a bad writer, he can—I mean by that he could be a bad punctuator or grammarian—but he's still a first-rate writer if the people that he's portraying follow the universal patterns of man's behavior inside the human condition.

Q. Quite a few of the writers back in about 1900—when they would write a story such as about the meat packers in Chicago—would try to tell the story of individuals, but with a thought in mind that they saw an evil in society which should be corrected. Do you think, sir, that a writer has an obligation to try to point out through his stories an evil that he sees in a society or should he just tell a story of individuals and not try to make any generalization about society?

A. Let him stick to his story. If he feels that evil enough, he can't keep it out of the story. He don't have to make an effort to bring it in to show anyone. Let him stick to his story dealing with men and women in the human dilemma. If he feels that social evil enough, it will be there. That was the case of Sherwood Anderson and Sandburg and Dreiser and the other people writing in Chicago about that time—they were not propagandists on social evils. They couldn't keep the evil, the awareness of it, out, because it moved them as people. That was a part of their own dilemma.

Q. Sir, what do you think was the reason for the

exodus of the artists of America to Europe during the time of the Expatriates?

A. Probably a restlessness or itching feet as a result of the first war. That was the first time Americans in any quantity moved around much, went anywhere. And it was the legacy from the soldiers who had gone to strange lands, seen strange customs—an unrest, an upset. I think that's all that it was.

Q. Sir, last night you said that the youth of today have the same passions and desires that youth have always had. What is your opinion of the college student of today and the trouble he seems to get into in riots and this sort of thing? In your opinion, is this just an attempt to express himself, or just what do you believe it is?

A. Well, it could be. It could be a perfectly normal impulse to revolt. The riots and the troubles that students get into nowadays are not too different from the ones they were getting into back in 1900. There are just more of them. But the riots, the desires to protest, are still the same, and I think it's a force of youth that is misdirected. Now I won't say that, because I am not too sure it does any harm. Maybe it's a good safety valve. But it's a force that, if it could be directed into another channel, it could do something a little more— well, I don't like the word productive either.

Q. Sir, along the same line, do you feel that this reaction of youth, the juveniles of today, could be a result of not living what our hearts would have us live? In other words, the conformity of today? We are expected to react to certain pressures and to lead our lives in a certain way and go through high school, get our diplomas, go through college, dress the proper way, behave in the proper way. Do you feel that the outbursts of youth are the result of this sort of constriction or restrictions?

A.   I think that a great deal of it is a direct result of that. The trouble is that man is not to be pitied, but the generations of men have—can be born into an unfortunate time. I think that the pressure, the need to order the mass of humanity is a result of too many people and not enough room. If people are not more or less regimented, there won't be room for anyone to lift his elbow. And I think the young man and the young woman resents that. I would. Rightly. But, because there are too many people and less and less room, that is a condition which must obtain, and the young man and young woman must be tough enough to not let that make too much difference to him.

Q.   Sir, how serious do you think the problem of world over-population is?

A.   I think it is very serious.

Q.   Do you have any suggestions for a solution— anything that can be done now for this?

A.   Well, unless a law is passed that woman can't have but one child just like she can't have but one husband. That may come.

Q.   Sir, referring back to a question a moment ago, how would you redirect the energy of youth today? Would you attempt to do it as there has been an attempt to do it?

A.   I wouldn't like to see anyone attempt to direct the energies of youth. That's what Hitler did. That's what people like Hitler do. I think that there should be room for youth itself to decide where that energy wants to go instead of having to blow it off in a safety valve.

Q.   Sir, what about President Kennedy's Peace Corps? Do you think that this is a Hitler-type move? I mean it is voluntary now, but they are trying to direct the energies of youth.

A.   I don't believe that. I am not convinced that it will do a great deal of good, but I don't believe it will do the sort of harm that Hitler accomplished when he got hold of young people in Germany. I think that the difference is in the temperament of the German and the mixture of Anglo-Saxon and Latin and German which are us now.

Q.   Sir, concerning the South and the problem of segregation—you said that you thought the human being was always improving. Do you think that in the South there is a growing feeling that a man who has the ability despite whether he is black or white should have the same opportunity to compete and to excel in a job?

A.   I am inclined to think that with most people in the South that belief has been there all the time, but it's befogged by so much old, emotional inheritance that it is very difficult. It's hard for the Southerner to recognize that as simply and primarily a moral problem that has but one answer. It's very difficult to do that. It's a condition that will take a great deal of trying and trimming and fitting. It will cause a great deal more trouble and anguish. And I, myself, I wouldn't undertake to guess how many years it will be before the Negro has equality in my country, anything approaching equality. But I am convinced that the Negro is the one that will have to do it, not by getting enough white people on his side to pass laws and bayonets, but to make himself—to improve himself to where the white men in Mississippi say, will say, "Please join me." There is too much talk of right and not enough talk of responsibility in the whole thing.

Q. Sir, on the same subject of the South, what do you feel that the modern South is coming to in respect to industrialization—the movement of business from the North to the South? I would think that the tempo of life would have been speeded up somewhat.

A. Yes, it has, but then that change from the land to the town and the city is general through this country. It's not particularly unique to the South. It's only that the South is a little behind the rest of the country. But the same change is going on everywhere. In the South it will run into the old racial problems. But the same change is something that we have got to live with, to cope with. It's not Southern.

Q. How much are religion and sexual fear the basis of racial hatreds?

A. Well, there are some. But I think that basically what the people in the South are afraid of is the Negro vote. That if enough of him can vote, he will elect his own people or his own kind to office until some blackguard white man comes along and uses him again through his, the Negro's, ignorance. The Negro must—education is actually the solution, the only one which I can see. The Negro must be taught the principles of responsibility. In effect, for the next few years the Negro has got to be better than the white man. He has got to be more honest, more moral, because his color is against him. He's got to be the one that compels the white man to say, "Please join us."

Q.   Sir, we have talked today a great deal about the attitude of the American people towards war. This question is one we quite often hear around here. The question is simply, what do you feel should be the basic attitude of the American people towards the professional soldier? Do you feel that the professional soldier and a mighty army, such as President Kennedy seems to be advocating, are justified in view of the world situation, or are they merely a necessary evil or an outright evil.

A.   I would say that right now and until we know better, until conditions change, they are justified and damn necessary. But all life is in a constant flux. The only alternative to motion is stasis—death. And these conditions must change. It would be nice if we had a constant new crop of leaders trained for leadership coming up as a constant new crop of military officers coming up all the time, instead of using government as a refuge for your indigent kinfolks as we are prone to do in this country. A man can't make a living any other way, we elect him to something.

Q.   Sir, I was wondering about the type of government we have here in the United States. We seem to be working toward an objective we have stated in our Constitution, and we feel that this is the best form of government. We have tried to put this into other countries in Asia and in Europe, and yet they seem to fail in a great many instances. Do you think that possibly this form of government is unique to countries of western and northern Europe and the Americas and cannot be applied to countries in Southeast Asia and the Middle East?

A. I would hate to believe that. I think that our mistake is that we don't try to educate the people in the foreign countries to know enough about the sort of government that we attempt to force on them. I would not like to believe that certain people are ethnologically incapable of democracy. I would like to believe that all people are, but I do think that people have got to be educated to it. I think that we got educated to it through the hardship that we went through in the early times of our Revolution. I think that at that time we were fortunate in the leaders that came to the top were not the people like the Chinese and the Russian peoples. I don't believe that we are any wiser or more sensible than Russians or Chinese. I would hate to think that only the Anglo-Saxon is competent for democracy. It looks like it, but that's only the ephemeral condition of today, which will pass.

Q. Sir, in view of our world situation, in view of what you said about the fact that man will straighten himself out, do you feel that it should be the role of the

United States to initiate a move towards a lessening of international tensions by unilateral disarmament or maybe a little closer cooperation? Do you feel that this is part of the answer?

A. I am not too sure that all the summit talks and the foreign ministers' talks ever do much good, but I don't think they do any harm. And certainly as long as people talk, they don't fight.

———————

Between classes, Mr. Faulkner paid an office call on the Superintendent; then at 9:30 A.M., he went back to the classroom to converse with two other sections of cadets.

EN 152: The Evolution of American Ideals as Reflected in American Literature

9:30 A.M.–10:25 A.M., April 20, 1962

――――――

Q. Could you tell us, Mr. Faulkner, exactly what qualities Don Quixote has that make him one of your favorite characters?

A. It's admiration and pity and amusement—that's what I get from him—and the reason is that he is a man trying to do the best he can in this ramshackle universe he's compelled to live in. He has ideals which are by our—the pharisaical standards are nonsensical. But by my standards they are not nonsensical. His method of trying to put them into practice is tragic and comic. I can see myself in Don Quixote by reading a page or two now and then, and I would like to think that my behavior is better for having read *Don Quixote.*

Q. Mr. Faulkner, there have been several comments recently concerning your style. I am thinking specifically of your sentence structure, in which you seem to have run-on sentences consisting possibly of twenty-six or twenty-seven lines, and also of your vague pronoun references. By vague pronoun reference I am thinking of the first five or six pages of *Intruder in the Dust*. When you speak of a "he" and do not refer to the subject of this "he," I wonder if you have any special purpose in doing this, or is this just the result of the thoughts in your mind as you are trying to express your thoughts?

A. The germ of it was a special purpose—not at all to be obscure. I think that any artist, musician, writer, painter would like to take all of the experience which he has seen, observed, felt and reduce that to one single color or tone or word, which is impossible. In fact, he would like to reduce all human experience onto the head of a pin as the man engraved the Lord's Prayer on the head of a pin once. He can't do that, but he is still going to try. And the obscurity, the prolixity which you find in writers is simply that desire to put all that experience into one word. Then he has got to add another word, another word becomes a sentence, but he's still trying to get it into one unstopping whole—a paragraph or a page—before he finds a place to put a full stop. The style—I think the story the writer is trying to tell invents, compels its style. That no writer has got the time to be obscure for the sake of obscurity. It's because at that moment he couldn't think of any better way to tell the story he was trying to tell.

Q. Sir, do you believe that the events in an author's life have any significant effect upon his writing?

A. I think that every experience of the author affects his writing. That he is amoral or thief, he will rob and steal from any and every source; he will use everything; everything is grist to his mill from the telephone book up or down, and naturally all his own experience is stored away. He has a sort of a lumber room in his subconscious that all this goes into, and none of it is ever lost. Some day he may need some experience that he experienced or saw, observed or read about, and so he digs it out and uses it. I don't think he gets off to suffer experience just to use it. But everything that happens to him he remembers. And it will be grist to his mill.

Q. Sir, I just finished reading *As I Lay Dying*. You stated last night that there are three things that a person, a writer, may draw upon in order to get his ideas for a story. One was imagination, another was experience, and the third was observation. I would like to know where you got the idea for *As I Lay Dying*.

A. They are people that I have known all my life in the country I was born in. The actions, the separate actions, I may have seen, remembered. It was the imagination probably that tied the whole thing together into a story. It's difficult to say just what part of any story comes specifically from imagination, what part from experience, what part from observation. It's like having—as I said last night—three tanks with a collector valve. And you don't know just how much comes from which tank. All you know is a stream of water runs from the valve when you open it, drawn from the three tanks—observation, experience, imagination.

Q. Sir, I would like to know if at present you have any ideas concerning what you are going to write in the future. Do you have any feelings that you feel you would like to put down on paper sometimes in the future or that you are working on right now?

A. No, a disorderly writer like me is incapable of making plans and plots. He writes simply about people, and the story begins with a phrase, an anecdote, or a gesture, and it goes from there and he tries to stop it as soon as he can. If he can stop it in ten pages, he does. If it needs a hundred pages, it demands a hundred pages. But it's not done with any plan or schedule of work tomorrow. I am simply writing about people, man in his comic or tragic human condition, in motion, to tell a story—give it some order and unity and coherence—that to me seems tragic or funny.

Q. Sir, I would like to know if you could tell us where and when you first learned to give these stories of yours this unity and coherence and meaning. Was there some definite time of your life in which this was taught to you or you learned it?

A. I learned it by what seems to me necessity. I was the oldest of four brothers, and we had certain chores—milking and feeding and things like that to do at home—and I found pretty soon that if I told stories the others did the work. That was when I begun to dabble in fiction. And I could get boys from the neighborhood in when there was a lot of work to be done, get that done too—I sort of contracted out, you see.

Q. Do you think an American author, Mr. Faulkner, has to have another job besides writing?

A. Yes, I do. I think any author should because, if you are not careful, you'll begin to think of the work you do in terms of how much you can make. And everybody likes a little money for tobacco and whiskey and a little fun occasionally besides something to eat. And it's best to have a job so that the writer can remain an amateur all the time; never let the writing get involved with earning the daily bread. So I think that any writer should have another job, unless he is rich.

Q. Sir, in regard to the racial incidents in the last few years, such as freedom riders and school integrationists, do you believe that they have any day-to-day effect on Southern institutions, or are the Southern institutions just going to change in gradual evolution?

A. It's a part of the change, and I think that any condition, situation, human living situation will have to change because life is motion and the only alternative to motion is stasis—death. It's bound to change whether we like it or not. It will change. These are the ephemeral symptoms of the unrest which take unhappy—bring about unhappy, unfortunate situations, but I don't think that they either help or impede the progress of change, which is inevitable and will occur.

Q. Sir, when you are actually putting something on paper, do you let yourself flow out freely until you, say, feel temporarily empty, or do you have to force yourself to write for an extended period of time?

A. I have, myself, one simple rule, which is to write it only when it is hot, and always stop before it cools off so I will have something to go back to; never to write myself out. But there is somewhere, whether you realize it or not, there is the policeman that insists on some order, some unity in the work. But I would say to never force yourself to write anything. Once you do that you begin to think, "Well, I might as well force myself to write something and make a little money out of it." And then you are sunk—you are gone, you have stopped being a writer. You must be an amateur writer always. You must do it because it's fun, just like you play a hard set of tennis because it's fun, not for profit—because it's your cup of tea.

Q. Sir, do you consider such controversial works as *Tropic of Cancer* and *Lolita* good literature, or do you consider them just a collection of sordid incidents written for money?

A. I wouldn't undertake a judgment until I read the book. I haven't read that book yet. I would like to read it before I decide. I would give anyone the benefit of the doubt and assume that he is primarily trying to tell me a story rather than to titillate me.

Q. Sir, right after the First World War there was a group of American writers who went to France, the Expatriates. I'd like to know if you, at the time, had any opinion about their journey to France from America—why they went and what they did.

A. That came up this morning in the other class. I think in the War, 1917–18, is the first time that Americans ever really did much traveling to any extent in great numbers. And the exodus to Europe among writers afterwards was still a part of the same unrest. They had—some of them had been soldiers and found out that life in Europe was different and was pleasant and they went back to it. But I think it was part of the whole seethe, that unrest that suddenly got us involved in a war that many miles away which is still going on. I don't mean the war but the seethe, the unrest, the movement. And they—the writer, the artist is quite often the venturesome one, and he was the vanguard of the exodus, the trek back and forth to Europe.

Instructor: Perhaps, sir, you would comment to this class, as you did to the last, on the difference in the attitudes toward war of Midshipman Hope and Captain Bogard in "Turnabout"—the young British midshipman who treated war as a game as opposed to the very serious American captain.

A. Yes, I believe what I said was that it was a contrast not of nationalities so much as age. The British midshipman was only seventeen or eighteen years old—should still have been in school. The American captain was a mature man, and the American captain survives where the seventeen-year-old midshipman didn't, possibly because maturity will help a man to survive in a crisis. That the soldier who has a little maturity—a little—not so much experience but the discipline to stop and weigh what he's doing, where he is, may survive where the younger man who is no less brave or no more brave will lose his life—if that story did prove anything like that—I think that was. . . .

Instructor: Of course, I am sure most of the cadets now realize that we taught the story, or we discussed it, from the standpoint of attempting to infer about national characteristics or national attitudes from these two people and were completely wrong.

A. Yes, I don't think that national characteristics, attitudes, are important, and I am inclined to think now that they are dangerous if you pay too much attention to them. That people have got to be people first, whether they like it or not.

Q. Sir, would you say that the bravado the young midshipman had is better in a way than the courage which the captain possessed in a mature manner, and that actually the older man was influenced by the young man? Later on in the story the captain does dive his plane toward a house almost to the point of collision.

A. Well, they were national traits. The swagger and the *insouciance* of the midshipman were British traits; the captain's colder, considering courage was typical of a Yale Skull and Bones man, which he was. I think that when he dove his bomber down on the roofs of that chateau, it was a gesture of revolt against all the brass-bound stupidity of the generals and admirals that sit safe in the dugouts and tell the young men to go there and do that. That that was something that probably every soldier in war has felt. They have cursed the whole lot of them—that my brother is the man I am trying to kill. But you people safe at home—curse all of them. I am sure every soldier has felt that.

Q. Sir, in your short story "Beyond," I was wondering what the young child with the wounds in his hands and his feet represented.

A. That was probably allegorical, symbolical, out of the background of religion which we all have and which is a part of the experience the writer draws from without deliberately trying to draw a parallel between this child and Christ—it's there, and if it seems good at the moment, he uses it with all gratitude—with all circumspection he will use it.

Q. Sir, what is your purpose in the revision of "The Bear," the short story about the boy and the large outlaw bear?

A. It was not really revised. It was a necessary portion of what to me was not a collection of short stories, but a novel, a book [*Go Down, Moses*]. And it seemed to me that it was necessary to break the story of the bear at one point and put something else in for the same reason that the musician says, "Now at this point I will need counterpoint. I will need discord. Or I will suspend this theme for another." It seems right for him to do. That was the reason. The story, if you drop out the—I think it's the third or fourth section, is just as I wrote it.

Q. Mr. Faulkner, I was just wondering if there was any personal experience involved in the inspiration of the events that transpired between the boy and the bear in that story.

A. Well, that was a part of my youth, my childhood, too. My father and his friends owned leases on the land similar to that. And I was taken there as soon as I was big enough to go into the woods with a gun, and I don't remember now just how much of that might have been actual, how much I invented. The three-toed bear was an actual bear. But I don't know that anyone killed him with a knife. And the dog was an actual dog, but I don't remember that they ever came into juxtaposition. It's difficult to say. That's the case of the three tanks with the collector. The writer's too busy to know whether he is stealing or lying. He's simply telling a story.

Q. Sir, last night you made a statement that you yourself write to tell a story, primarily. And you write it the best way possible and as vividly and as descriptively as possible. Do you believe that most authors are bound by this rule or that they do have some motive such as teaching a lesson or, to put it tritely, that they have a phrase, "The moral of the story is . . . "?

A. I am inclined to believe that we all write for the same reason. There can be a writer who has been so harried and so outraged by a social condition that he can't keep that social condition out of his story. But he is primarily telling a story of man struggling in the human condition—not a sociological condition but the condition of the heart's dilemma. I don't believe that he realizes until after that he has preached a sermon too. I think that he was primarily telling a story.

Q. Sir, along this same line, would you say that books such as *Uncle Tom's Cabin* would be written because of sociological conditions?

A.   I would say that *Uncle Tom's Cabin* was written out of violent and misdirected compassion and ignorance of the author toward a situation which she knew only by hearsay. But it was not an intellectual process, it was hotter than that; it was out of her heart. It just happened that she was telling a story of Uncle Tom and the little girl, not telling the story—not writing a treatise on the impressions of slavery, because everybody knows that slaves have always had a hard time of it, not just Negro slaves in America, but the whole history back in Biblical times. She was simply writing a story which moved her, seemed so terrible and so hot to her that it had to be told. But I think she was writing about Uncle Tom as a human being—and Legree and Eliza as human beings, not as puppets.

Q.   Sir, I would like to know exactly what it was that inspired you to become a writer.

A.   Well, I probably was born with the liking for inventing stories. I took it up in 1920. I lived in New Orleans, I was working for a bootlegger. He had a launch that I would take down the Pontchartrain into the Gulf to an island where the rum, the green rum, would be brought up from Cuba and buried, and we would dig it up and bring it back to New Orleans, and he would make scotch or gin or whatever he wanted. He had the bottles labeled and everything. And I would get a hundred dollars a trip for that, and I didn't need much money, so I would get along until I ran out of money again. And I met Sherwood Anderson by chance, and we took to each other from the first. I'd meet him in the afternoon, we would walk and he would talk and I would listen. In the evening we would go somewhere to a speakeasy and drink, and he would talk and I would listen. The next morning he would say, "Well I have to work in the morning," so I wouldn't see him until the next afternoon. And I thought if that's the sort of life writers lead, that's the life for me. So I wrote a book and, as soon as I started, I found out it was fun. And I hadn't seen him and Mrs. Anderson for some time until I met her on the street, and she said, "Are you mad at us?" and I said, "No, ma'am, I'm writing a book," and she said, "Good Lord!" I saw her again, still having fun writing the book, and she said, "Do you want Sherwood to see your book when you finish it?" and I said, "Well, I hadn't thought about it." She said, "Well, he will make a trade with you; if he don't have to read that book, he will tell his publisher to take it." I said, "Done!" So I finished the book and he told Liveright to take it and Liveright took it. And that was how I became a writer—that was the mechanics of it.

Instructor: Would you recommend any specific works for these aspiring soldiers to read, sir, or would you recommend a particular sequence of your works that might help them in an approach to your novels?

A. To my notion, literature is such a pleasant thing, having kept it amateur, that I wouldn't advise anyone to read or write either as a job or duty. But I would say that, read everything. It don't matter what it is. Trash, the best, the worst, read everything. And if anyone does want to be a writer, he certainly must learn his craft, and the best way to learn it is from the people who can do it well. But I would read for pleasure and I would write for pleasure—not for money, not as a duty.

Q. Sir, do you have any particular reason for making some of your books a collection of short stories and another book a novel?

A. Yes, there must be some reason. In some cases the short stories, though they fall into the form of short stories, are to me continuous chapters in what is actually a novel. In other cases they are simply a collection of short stories in order to collect [them] into a book. As I said, I think that any writer wants to put down the magic of breathing in one word if he can, in a sonnet if he can, in a short story if he can, then in a novel if he must. But he is not too interested in the form it finally takes as a book. He is simply trying to get it down and get it said, and he would like to say it in one word if he could, which is impossible. It's like a jewel.

Q. Sir, did you have any particular reason for choosing the work that you read last night?

A. Yes, I had spoken to my son-in-law, Summers, who was here, class of '51, and I asked him what he would like to hear a middle-aged writer read when he was here, and he said he thought it should be from the current work, the one I just finished. I asked Major Fant about it, and Major Fant agreed. So that was sort of a unanimous opinion that's what we would read.

Q. Sir, I understand during your stay here you have been observing cadet life a little bit, especially at reveille. What is your opinion of the freshman or Fourth Class System?

A.   Now, I don't know enough about it to be—to express opinions like that. But I have a different idea of the sort of men that are here from what I had when I came. I had expected a certain rigidity of—not thinking—but of the sort of questions I would get. And I was pleasantly astonished to find that the questions I got came from human beings, not from third classmen or second classmen or first classmen, but from human beings, from young men that had an idea that maybe a gray-headed bloke like me knew answers, and [could] answer the question. But I assume that your system— Fourth Class System—is a good one or they wouldn't have it.

Q.   Sir, some of the remarks you made last night when you were reading showed a knowledge of the terms used around a race track. Do you ever research any of your topics?

A.   No, that's out of observation, all the horse business more or less from experience. My father was a horseman, I have lived among horses all my life and still own horses and hunt in Virginia. And I have lost enough money at race tracks to know something about the jargon.

Q.   Sir, could you tell us something about your grandfather? I understand that he was an interesting man and may have had some influence on your writing.

A.   Yes, he was. He came into Mississippi on foot when he was fourteen years old. Ran away from home in Virginia looking for a distant relation—found him. At the moment his uncle was in jail for having shot a man. He—well, the story is that he saw a young girl in a yard that he passed and said, "When I get big I am going to marry her." And he did. That is, all this is the sort of thing that any hack writer might invent, you see, as a character. But later he got into politics. He went to the Mexican War as a friend of Jefferson Davis. In 1860 he organized, raised, and paid most of the expenses for the Second Mississippi Infantry and came to Virginia as its colonel. He commanded, as senior colonel, the brigade with Jackson until Bee arived and took command before First Manassas. He went back after the—in the election of officers the next year at Opequon Creek—he was a martinet, and his men elected his lieutenant colonel to command the regiment, and my grandfather got mad and went back to Mississippi, and got bored after a while and raised a company of partisan cavalry that was finally brigaded into Forrest, and he finished the war there as a cavalryman. And later got in politics and made some money. He built a railroad there—the first railroad in the country. He made the grand tour in Europe, and then he took to writing books, and I may have inherited the ink stain from him. He was killed in a duel before I was born.

Q. Sir, there has been a lot of talk recently about goals for America, and the President has appointed a commission to study this. Do you believe that it is necessary for a nation to have a certain set of defined goals, or do you feel that an individual should go along by himself?

A.   I think if the individual takes care of himself and his own goals and his own conscience, that his nation will be in pretty good shape.

Q.   Sir, in your book *The Sound and the Fury*, in the first part things are seen through the eyes of the idiot Benjy. Why do you do this?

A.   That was that same hope that I tried to express that the artist feels to condense all experiences onto the head of the pin. That began as the story of a funeral. It's first—the first thing I thought of was the picture of the muddy seat of that little girl's drawers climbing the pear tree to look in the parlor window to see what in the world the grown people were doing that the children couldn't see, and I decided that the most effective way to tell that would be through the eyes of the idiot child who didn't even know, couldn't understand what was going on. And that went on for a while, and I thought it was going to be a ten-page short story. The first thing I knew I had about a hundred pages. I finished, and I still hadn't told that story. So I chose another one of the children, let him try. That went for a hundred pages, and I still hadn't told that story. So I picked out the other one, the one that was the nearest to what we call sane to see if maybe he could unravel the thing. He talked for a hundred pages, he hadn't told it, then I let Faulkner try it for a hundred pages. And when I got done, it still wasn't finished, and so twenty years later I wrote an appendix to it, tried to tell that story. That's all I was doing on the first page, was trying to tell what to me seemed a beautiful and tragic story of that doomed little girl climbing the pear tree to see the funeral.

Q.   Sir, along these lines, when you first begin to write a story, do you have sort of an outline in your mind of what the whole story is going to consist of or do you sort of develop it as you write?

A.   I would say it develops itself. It begins with a character, usually, and once he stands up on his feet and begins to move, all I do is to trot along behind him with a paper and pencil trying to keep up long enough to put down what he says and does, that he is taking charge of it. I have very little to do except the police-man in the back of the head which insists on unity and coherence and emphasis in telling it. But the characters themselves, they do what they do, not me.

Q.   Why did you have so much trouble trying to end *The Sound and the Fury*? If an author has some-thing in his heart that he has to get down on paper, why is it such a struggle to bring it about?

A.   He wants to make it on paper as startling, as comic, anyway as moving, as true, as important as it seems in the imagination. And in the process of getting it into cold words on the paper, something escapes from it. It's still not as good as when he dreamed it. Which is the reason that when he finishes that to the best of his ability, he writes, tries again—he writes another one. He is still trying to capture that dream, that image of man, either victorious or defeated, in some splendid, beautiful gesture inside the dilemma of the human heart.

Q. Sir, I was wondering if you read much of the criticism that is written about your own work.

A. Don't read any of it. I'd rather read my fiction at firsthand, I think.

Q. Sir, have you ever desired to be anything besides a writer?

A. Why sure, I'd like to be a brave, courageous soldier; I have thought of all sorts of things I'd like to be. I'd like to be a beautiful woman. I'd like to be a millionaire.

Q. Sir, we have a paper downstairs in an English display which comments on Robert Frost's impression of Mr. Khrushchev. Mr. Frost has a rather favorable impression of this man. What is your opinion of such a personality as Mr. Khrushchev?

A. Probably my opinion of Mr. Khrushchev is the same one the newspapers and what I read have given me. I know too little about him. I have my doubts of that whole system and I—and since I doubt, that whole system, I would doubt anyone it spewed up to the top, no matter who he was. But I know too little to have an opinion that's worth expressing—that is, any opinion I express would have to be, how to say it, from up here [pointing to his head], not from here [pointing to his heart].

Q. Sir, you place your stories against a whole host of different backgrounds, and I was wondering what background you yourself are happiest in, that you feel most at home in.

A. Well, almost anywhere. I am something like a cat probably. One place is the same as another to me. I get along, as far as I know, quite well with all sorts of people. There's a—some reasons that some time of the year I like Virginia because they have the fox hunting that I like there; at other times of the year I like Mississippi because there are things I like there. In the background that the writer uses in his story, he simply uses the one he is most familiar with, so that he won't have to do a lot of research. People behave the same. But you might make little mistakes of dialect or custom that someone from Cape Cod would say, "Uh-uh, us folks don't act like that up here," but if you are located in the country you are familiar with nobody can check you on it. You don't have to be careful.

Q. Sir, you stated last night that one of the primary sources that a writer gets his ideas from is someone else's books—reading. Do you just pick something up as you go along, something that interests you, or do you have a schedule of reading?

A. No, I never have. When I was young I was an omniverous reader with no judgment, no discretion—I read everything. As I have gotten along in years, I don't read with the same voracity, and I go to the book as you go to spend a few minutes with a friend you like. I will open the book to a particular chapter or to read about a particular character in it. Not to read the book but just to spend a little while with a human being that I think is funny or tragic or anyway interesting.

Q. Last night you said, sir, it was a writer's duty

to portray the feelings and emotions of the human heart. Well, what books, other than some of your own works, do you feel best do this?

A. Well, almost all do, except the ones that are untruthful and shabby and are simply written to titilate and to make money. Almost any book you open will do that—anything in Shakespeare, Tolstoy, Dostoevsky, Balzac, Gautier, Dreiser, Lewis, Anderson. There are problems which you recognize at once as being familiar problems, that is so familiar, or familiar enough to— where you say, "Yes, I believe that's so, I believe that's true, that this is what I felt or what I imagine myself feeling. I would know this anguish. Anyway, I believe this anguish is so."

Q. Sir, what do you think are the outstanding traits of the South as a region?

A. Do you mean the ones that are the most noticeable or the ones that you would like the best?

Q. Well, both of them, sir.

A. Well, the most noticeable trait is belief that we can repeal 1962. I would think that the trait I like best is of courtesy, of automatic courtesy. That is, you say, "Thank you," and "Sir," and "Ma'am," to anyone— everyone—regardless whether—hospitality. I don't like the emotionalism, the propensity to depend on the emotions instead of on the gray matter. I don't like the hot summers. I have said for sixty-five years I'd never spend another summer there, and yet I am going back in June.

Q. Sir, what is your attitude to having motion pictures made of your works?

A. Well, it's a good way to make a little money. I have in the contract that I don't have to see the picture, so it never confuses me, and I spend the money, sometimes wisely—but anyway it's nice to have a little money now and then.

Q. Sir, do you reread your old works?

A. Yes, just as I will reread into certain pages of Dickens to spend time with people that I like or are funny. I like my sewing machine agent Ratliff, I will go back to read about him, to laugh again quite often, just as I read about Sarah Gamp, just as I read into *Don Quixote*.

Q. Mr. Faulkner, in *Knight's Gambit* there is a character named Monk, who was an imbecile. Exactly how did you create him?

A. I can remember a country man in my county that looked like him, who was half-witted, and possibly the story came from that. This man, a half-wit, harmless, but with no future, nothing to be done—and so possibly I tried to invent a future, even a tragic one for him, something to leave his mark on the world instead of living and dying a harmless half-imbecile. That's a case—it's difficult to say just where you get the idea, it may be from something you saw—then you won't let it alone. Certainly I don't think that any writer ever wrote down or put down anything he actually saw or heard because a writer is congenitally incapable of telling the truth about anything. He has got to change it. He has got to lie. That's why they call it fiction, you see.

Q. Sir, what do you consider to be the qualities

that an imbecile or half-wit possesses that enables him to see stories in the way that you are looking for?

A. I wouldn't say that he had those qualities. That is the prerogative of the writer to use his imagination to that extent if it makes something that seems moving and true. Maybe the imbecile should have that quality. That's what I mean by truth. He probably hasn't, which is the fact, but maybe he should, which is the truth.

Q. Sir, why were you so apparently anxious to involve yourself in the First World War? You were rejected by the American Army and you joined up with the Canadian. Were you just restless or curious?

A. Sure, something going on. Folks in Mississippi didn't get to travel much. There was a chance to travel free. Of course, when you are seventeen or eighteen you don't have any more sense that that, you know.

Q. A lot of people, sir, have commented on the present state of American morals and say that we are going to the dogs in certain ways. Do you believe that our morals have actually been diluted that much from what they were years ago?

A. The first thing I can remember hearing my Grandmother and my maiden aunt say is, that young people are going to the dogs. That was back in about 1904 or '05 and probably young people always will be going to the dogs; there will always be somebody seventy or eighty years old to notice it and tell you about it. I was going to say that there is probably more juvenile delinquency today because there are more juveniles.

Q. Do you think the period of the Depression has

had very much effect on literature, on the stories people wanted to tell?

A. Only—it has changed the outside pattern of what they want. It hasn't change what they did. It hasn't changed the passions and hopes that drove them to the actions. It would appear in the story as the coincidence of the environment, not as any alteration in the hope, the striving of the particular human heart, because the dilemma is the same one. It has nothing to do with depression or segregation. The dilemmas are a little more eternal than that.

Q. As a general rule, sir, can someone find your attitude towards a subject by examining the attitude of some of your characters in your stories?

A. Probably a lot of people have tried that. I think that any book should have on the first page, "The author declines to accept responsibility for the behavior or actions or speeches of any of these characters, because he is simply trying to tell you a story." And these people that he uses, they don't necessarily have to believe as he believes. He quite often hates them, disagrees with them. But they seem to him necessary to tell the story which he is trying to tell.

Q. Sir, what is your evaluation of poetry as the means of expressing the human heart?

A. To me, poetry is first. The failed poet becomes a short story writer. The failed short story writer has nothing left but the novel, so he's a novelist. But poetry, to me, is first. That is the nearest approach to condensing all the beauty and passion of the human heart onto the head of the pin.

Q. Sir, do you actually believe it is possible then to communicate the feeling of one person to another person, completely?

A. Yes, you don't necessarily need to depend on words to do it, but, yes, I think people can communicate.

Q. I mean, sir, do you believe it is actually possible to give a completely accurate communication?

A. Yes, possible. But it is not always deliberately possible—that is, you can't sit down—I am going to communicate a thought to you, so here it is. I think that that is by accident, the communication comes across a long distance and maybe years later through something that neither party believed was going to carry the message.

Q. Sir, during your writing do you ever become discouraged with your work, or have you always felt that you were enjoying this to the utmost and that you would always write throughout the rest of your life? In other words, have you ever become discouraged in your work at any time?

A. Yes, constantly. That's why writing is such a matchless vocation to follow. It never gives you any peace. The discouragement is because it ain't quite as good as that dream, it ain't quite as good as you want it to be—you are frustrated, you are enraged at it. You tear it up, burn it, but you don't quit. As soon as you cool off a little, then you try it again, because there is nothing that can match the pleasure of creation—of creating some form of art, because only that way can you affirm your immortality. That all any artist is trying to do is, he knows that after a few years he will pass through the final gate into oblivion. He is simply going to leave on that wall "Kilroy was here." Not for power, not for money, but simply to say "I was here for a little while, I left this mark."

Q. Sir, many times in their works, authors include characters which are said to be either autobiographical or to represent a close relative or friend. Are these characters ever put in there purposely to represent these people or is it just telling a story and they just happen to coincide with real people?

A. As I said a while ago, the writer is incapable of telling the truth. He couldn't take an actual human being and translate him onto paper and stick to the facts. He has got to change and embroider. And he will—he is completely ruthless about that. He will alter the known human being out of all recognition if it suits his purpose, because he is simply not trying to portray that human being but to tell you a story of that human being moving—in motion.

Q. You speak, sir, of human immorality and at the same time you say that man will pass into oblivion. Now, I don't quite understand what you mean by that.

A. Well, the individual—you and I know that after a certain time we will be no more. Where we will be then we don't know yet. But we do know that at a certain time we will be no more. That's what I meant by the mortality of the individual. The immortality is the fact that frail, fragile man, a web of bone and nerves, mostly water, in a ramshackle universe has outlasted most other forms of mammalian life. He has outlasted his own disasters, and I think that he will continue— that, for the reason I believe I said this morning, that the species which has created the fine picture, the music, the statues, the books, is too valuable for omnipotence, God whoever he is, to let perish. That is the immortality of the race, not of the individual.

Q. Sir, then you feel that evolution, the mammalian evolution, ceases with the human being, that we couldn't possibly die out and something better take our place?

A. I don't know. I wouldn't make a statement like that, nobody would, actually. We don't know what man might evolve into—just how low he is, what flea he is on something that we can't even see, it is so great, so vast.

Q. Sir, if that small child in your story "Beyond" represented religion, why would you portray him as just a small child who is always crying and dirty and lacking self-control?

A. I didn't say that he represented religion. I said that, if I had put holes in his hands and feet, it was very likely a symbolism out of my religious background from the image of the Christ—that I wasn't trying to show up the Chirst at all. I simply, at that moment, felt that my story needed the symbolism which I could borrow from the history of the crucifixion or the marks of the crucifixion on this child. I would have to read the story again to probably answer you more, because I don't remember the story. That was a long time ago.

Q. Sir, the essay seems to be entirely foreign to your style of writing and thinking as a form of literature. Have you ever had any experience at essay writing, or what's your opinion of yourself writing an essay?

A. Well, my opinion is that that's not for me, that I don't have enough education, I don't know anything about ideas, to write an essay. All I know about are people in the seethe and the fury of the human condition, in motion. Like all uneducated people, I have a certain distrust of ideas. I think that, if I had to depend on something, I would depend on what my heart tells me, not on what my mind tells me, because I have no confidence in my brain.

Q. Sir, a little while back you made the statement that you rank poetry as the first form of literature, then short stories, then the novel. Around here, sir, in our English Department, we find that we are to write clearly and concisely in as few words as possible. Is this why perhaps you rank the short story ahead of the novel?

A. It's not why, but they go along with each other. What you are taught about preciseness and brevity is exactly what the poet has learned to practice, only the poet can cast over it such a magic that you can see the picture of all human passion in the fourteen lines of the sonnet. That's the magic of his talent, but the conciseness is exactly what you are trained [in] here. It's to say it in one word, if possible, which is what the poet wants to do. It can't be done, so he takes fourteen lines.

After this classroom session, Mr. Faulkner went to Colonel Alspach's office where Henri Cartier-Bresson, on assignment for *Vogue,* and Carl Mydans,[1] of *Life,* took a series of photographs. While these were being taken Colonel Alspach asked Mr. Faulkner about Joanna Burden in *Light in August:* "Isn't she kin to some of Hawthorne's people, like what Goodman Brown dreamed his wife was; and kin to Kurtz in *Heart of Darkness?*" Mr. Faulkner nodded. "Remember, sir," he said, "Joanna Burden had New England ancestry."

At lunch, Brigadier General Richard G. Stilwell, the Commandant of Cadets, was host to Mr. Faulkner and Mr. Summers in the Cadet Dining Hall. When it was announced by the Cadet First Captain that Mr. Faulkner was present, thunderous applause broke out.

Before the departure of the Faulkner party from West Point, Major Fant asked Mr. Faulkner if there was anything else he'd like to see. "No, sir," he responded. "I think I've seen enough. I'll just let it gestate a while."

---

[1] Mr. Mydans was asked why he took so many pictures. "Because," he replied, "this is not just a great man, this is a very great man."

Mr. and Mrs. William Faulkner at Stewart Air Force Base, New York, before departing for Charlottesville, Virginia, April 20, 1962.

Appendix

Oxford, Miss.
10 Feb. 1962

Dear General Westmoreland:

Your letter of Feb. 1st. has teached
me here. Mrs Faulkner and Mr and Mrs Summers (Summers
was class of '51 I believe) would like very much to
come along; I think Mr Summers has already been in
communication with the Major Professorof English,
whom he knew while at the Academy.

That is, I hope Mr Summers explained
that I am not a finished lecturer but am rather a
conversationalist, better at ousetion-and-answer sessions than as a speaker.

This is to ratify the date of to April
19th. The aircraft will be met at the Charlottesville
airport at whatever hour the Captain of it sets for
arrival or departure, if he will notify me at the
Charlottesville address.

Thank you for the invitation, and the
inclusion of Mrs Faulkner and Mr and Mrs Summers.

Respectfully,

William Faulkner

Wm Faulkner

Oxford, Miss.
25 June, 1962

Dear General Westmoreland:

It is with pleasure and pride too that
I hold in my hands the handsome log-book in which is
recorded my visit to the Academy---a visit not just
memorable for the honor it conferred on me, but for
the many and unfailing courtesies with which the four
of us---Mrs Faulkner and myself and our son and daugh-
ter---were surrounded.

One pleasure was of course a private one.
That was watching our youngest daughter being fetched
back to visit his alma mater by her husband (Paul Summers, class of '51), not as a guest of the class of
ø '51 but among the very top brass hats themselves.

Please accept for the Staff and Corps
the grateful thanks of Mrs Faulkner and myself and Mr
and Mrs Summers for the pleasure of our visit to the
Point, and to Mrs Westmoreland and yourself mine and
Mrs Faulkner's kindest personal regards.

Yours sincerely,

William Faulkner

William Faulkner

William Faulkner's speech of acceptance upon the award of the Nobel Prize for Literature, delivered in Stockholm on December 10, 1950.

I feel that this award was not made to me as a man, but to my work—a life's work in the agony and sweat of the human spirit, not for glory and least of all for profit, but to create out of the materials of the human spirit something which did not exist before. So this award is only mine in trust. It will not be difficult to find a dedication for the money part of it commensurate with the purpose and significance of its origin. But I would like to do the same with the acclaim too, by using this moment as a pinnacle from which I might be listened to by the young men and women already dedicated to the same anguish and travail, among whom is already that one who will some day stand here where I am standing.

Our tragedy today is a general and universal physical fear so long sustained by now that we can even bear it. There are no longer problems of the spirit. There is only the question: When will I be blown up? Because of this, the young man or woman writing today has forgotten the problems of the human heart in conflict with itself which alone can make good writing because only that is worth writing about, worth the agony and the sweat.

He must learn them again. He must teach himself that the basest of all things is to be afraid; and, teaching himself that, forget it forever, leaving no room in his workshop for anything but the old verities and truths of the heart, the old universal truths lacking which any story is ephemeral and doomed—love and honor and pity and pride and compassion and sacrifice. Until he does so, he labors under a curse. He writes not of love but of lust, of defeats in which nobody loses anything of value, of victories without hope and, worst of all, without pity or compassion. His griefs grieve on no universal bones, leaving no scars. He writes not of the heart but of the glands.

Until he relearns these things, he will write as though he stood among and watched the end of man. I decline to accept the end of man. It is easy enough to say that man is immortal simply because he will endure: that when the last ding-dong of doom has clanged and faded from the last worthless rock hanging tideless in the last red and dying evening, that even then there will still be one more sound: that of his puny inexhaustible voice, still talking. I refuse to accept this. I believe that man will not merely endure: he will prevail. He is immortal, not because he alone among creatures has an inexhaustible voice, but because he has a soul, a spirit capable of compassion and sacrifice and endurance. The poet's, the writer's, duty is to write about these things. It is his privilege to help man endure by lifting his heart, by reminding him of the courage and honor and hope and pride and compassion and pity and sacrifice which have been the glory of his past. The poet's voice need not merely be the record of man, it can be one of the props, the pillars to help him endure and prevail.

Reflections on Faulkner's visit, forty years later, by Joseph L. Fant III, Major General, USA Retired.

Two things make William Faulkner's visit to West Point important. First, as recorded in the preceding pages, the great detail, patience, and candor of his responses to cadet questions are unprecedented among Faulkner interviews. Second, in that he died two and a half months later, the views he so expansively shared with the cadets can be taken as representative of his opinions, his final word, on a great variety of subjects.

Faulkner at West Point has been translated into Dutch, Russian, and Japanese and twice into German. This second edition will be appreciated by Faulkner enthusiasts who do not own one of the four thousand original copies. There were a few points of interest about the visit not recorded in the first edition. Some of them follow.

At the dinner before Mr. Faulkner read to cadets, Mrs. Westmoreland, wife of General William C. Westmoreland, then the Superintendent of the Military Academy, mentioned having read that President and Mrs. Kennedy were going to host a dinner at the White House for all American Nobel laureates. She speculated that Faulkner would be excited by such an opportunity. He responded, "Ma'am, I'm not going to go." Surprised, she asked why not, and Faulkner replied, "Because I live in Charlottesville, ninety miles from Washington, and that's a fur piece to go for a meal." And he did not attend.

As we entered the foyer of South Auditorium, where Mr. Faulkner would speak, I noticed novelist Carson McCullers and asked Faulkner if he would like to speak to her. He assented, and after leading him to where she was standing, I rather inanely said, "Miss McCullers, may I present Mr. Faulkner." After my "introduction," she said, "I love your *The Sound and the Fury*." "Thank you, Ma'am," he replied, bowing slightly. "May I kiss you?" she asked. He did not respond, and she leaned forward and kissed him on the cheek—and that was the end of the encounter.

As we were en route to the airport where the party would board the plane for the trip back to Virginia, something triggered Mrs. Faulkner to chastise her husband for continually putting his boots on the mantel of whatever room in their house he might be in when he removed them. Having visited Rowan Oak a number of times since, I have noticed mantels in almost every room and cannot fail to visualize his muddy boots resting on each of them.

I am not sure how much tolerance today's Army extends to civilian periodicals, but in 1964 when publication of *Faulkner at West Point* was imminent, we were not permitted to accept $25,000 from *Esquire* magazine for a prepublication article of extracts because *Esquire* was considered "too risqué." We could well have used that money to help furnish the Faulkner Room in the cadet library, a space commemorating the visit and housing an impressive collection of Faulkner first editions, translations, and criticism of his work. I believe that Mr. Faulkner would have been pleased with the room.

One more point deserves mention. Besides providing a unique experience for our cadets, Mr. Faulkner's visit inspired the Department of English at the Military Academy to involve itself with *The Faulkner Concordance*, a twenty-one-year, twenty-eight-volume project initiated and directed by Brigadier General (USA Retired) Jack L. Capps with the assistance of several other officers and civilian scholars.

* * *

These glimpses, as well as the observations and comments recorded in the preceding record of the visit to West Point, characterize Mr. Faulkner's wit and personality. I remember him as more than a preeminent writer—rather as a sage for his vision in recognizing and succinctly expressing that many of the problems prevalent in our society, as certainly today as yesterday, are the results of "too much talk of right and not enough talk of responsibility." This statement and other of Faulkner's comments during his sessions with cadets confirm his status, so near the end of his life, as elder-statesman of American letters.

Reflections on Faulkner's visit, forty years later, by Daniel W. Christman, Lieutenant General, US Army, Superintendent, USMA.

April 20, 1962 dawned like every other day for a West Point plebe: a jumble of tasks to perform, information to memorize, and homework to complete. I prepared for duty as section marcher of my American literature class; as "section marcher," I was responsible for rendering the daily attendance report. But that day I eagerly anticipated one very special addition to my report: William Faulkner was coming to my class. I would sit next to a legend and have the opportunity to resolve a question that had been burning inside me since high school.

Exactly on schedule, at 0930, I rendered the report

to my instructor, Captain James Kintz, who along with Major Joe Fant made this course on American Ideals one of the most popular at USMA. And at the end of the table, sitting next to Captain Kintz, was William Faulkner. Within minutes I got my chance. As gingerly as a plebe could, I questioned Faulkner's unusual writing style at the beginning of *Intruder in the Dust*— particularly his tendency to employ vague pronoun references. I sought the answer that had eluded all of us in my high school literature class: why had he employed that style?

What I received back from Faulkner was much more than an answer to my question. He provided a primer on truth, about his requirement for honesty in character, fictional or real. Faulkner said simply that he was trying to portray the thoughts in his mind the best way he could, at the moment. Those thoughts, Faulkner elaborated, captured man's struggle with a universal condition, a condition defined by the conflicts of the human heart. He did not create his obscure style simply for the sake of obscurity, he said; there's no time for that. Instead, his style described, honestly and importantly, man "doing the best he can" in the universe in which he must live.

How glad I was to hear that studying Faulkner was more than analyzing eccentricities of style—and gladder still to learn that his style was a symptom of Faulkner's noble purpose rather than a shade obscuring it. For a plebe struggling through fourth class year, listening to Faulkner describe the hopes of man's heart was a welcome message indeed.

The spring of 1962 was a fascinating time to be a West Point cadet. In a span of less than forty days, many of us attended William Faulkner's reading, heard General MacArthur's "Duty, Honor, Country" address, and received John F. Kennedy's inspiring graduation message in early June. But no experience during my cadet career meant more than the quiet April hour I spent with a Nobel Prize winner. I stood in the presence of greatness—a greatness that inspired all of us to meet our own "conflicts of the heart" with the same optimism in mankind's future that Faulkner personified during his brief stay with us. It was a day I shall never forget.

About the Editors

JOSEPH L. FANT, at the time of Faulkner's visit, was an Assistant Professor of English at the United States Military Academy, from which he was graduated in 1951. Before returning to West Point to teach, he served in the Korean war, at various military posts throughout the United States, and in Germany.

ROBERT ASHLEY was Dean of the College and Professor of English at Ripon College. He was a member of the English Department at the United States Military Academy from 1951 to 1955. At the time of Faulkner's visit, he was a Lieutenant Colonel in the Army Reserve and was assigned to the Military Academy for his annual two weeks of active duty.

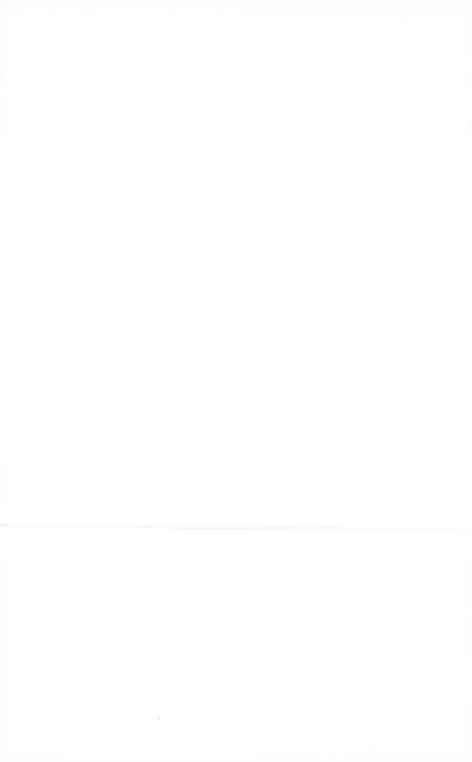